HEALTHY
SALADS FROM
SOUTHEAST ASIA

HEALTHY SALADS FROM SOUTHEAST ASIA

VATCHARIN BHUMICHITR

Photography by Gus Filgate

with additional photography by Michael Freeman
and Vatcharin Bhumichitr

WEATHERHILL

for my mother and father

Published in the United States by

Weatherhill, Inc.
41 Monroe Turnpike
Trumbull, CT 06611

in cooperation with

Kyle Cathie Limited
122 Arlington Road
London NW1 7HP

ISBN 0–8348–0498–0

1 3 5 7 9 8 6 4 2

Text © 2001 Vatcharin Bhumichitr
Project Editor: Lewis Esson
Designer: Geoff Hayes
Food for photography: Jane Suthering assisted by Olivier
Laudus, and Vatcharin Bhumichitr
Styling: Penny Markham
Food photography © Gus Filgate 2001
Travel photography on pages 4, 6/7, 9, 13, 14, 17, 18, 22,
28, 42/3, 56/7, 60, 70/71, 81, 86/7, 90, 91, 98/9, 104, 107,
112/3, 128/9, 136, 139, 142/3 © Michael Freeman 2001
Travel photography on pages 10, 15, 26/7, 37, 49, 117, 121
© Vatcharin Bhumichitr 2001

Vatcharin Bhumichitr is hereby identified as the author of this
work in accordance with Section 77 of the Copyright, Designs
and Patents Act 1988
A Cataloguing in Publication record for this title is available
from the British Library
Printed and bound in Singapore by Kyodo Printing Co.

Early morning, offering food to monks, a common sight across the whole of Buddhist Asia

contents

Every Wednesday, workers on my Aunt Chinda's farm in northern Thailand pack vegetables to be flown to Bangkok, where they will be delivered to the main luxury hotels. Her farm is in the foothills of the mountains just outside Chiang Mai, but the produce is not what you might expect – no bitter melon, lemon grass, sweet potato or other Oriental specialities. Indeed, at first glance the farmhands appear to be slicing and wrapping nothing but lettuces – but not quite. A closer look will reveal that these are actually rather unusual salad vegetables – rocket and radicchio, escarole and mustard greens, all bound for the smart French and Italian restaurants that now flourish in Bangkok, alongside the top Thai and Chinese restaurants.

Today, the European master chefs who come out for two or three years have to have these special ingredients and, when my aunt saw this potential market, she set up her farm to supply it. I played my part, buying seeds wherever I happened to be visiting – lamb's lettuce in France, spinach leaves in Italy – and posting them to her, often with little idea what I was sending, just a lot of gaudy leaves to judge by the packets. Now, when I see the lines of brightly coloured salad ingredients ready to be picked, I feel a – perhaps exaggerated – sense of achievement.

The farm workers themselves see nothing odd in this. Most still live in traditional wooden houses in hamlets dotted around the valley and, if you followed one of them home down one of the winding elephant tracks, you might be surprised to see him constantly stooping to pick plants and leaves, especially near the streams that bisect the valley floor, where plants grow in abundance. Of course, you would soon realize that our friend isn't collecting wild flowers, he is practising 'pick-and-cook' agriculture, a source of food as old as mankind and one still much in evidence all across Southeast Asia.

By the time he reaches home, his wife will have cooked sticky rice, the 'dry' variety that grows in forest clearings and which, when cooked, becomes glutinous or porridgy, unlike the more familiar 'wet' rice of the paddy regions, which is light and fluffy when steamed. She will have also prepared a spicy dip to accompany the expected plants, which will help send them and the rice down. So there it is, a perfect, easy and very cheap meal – rice, spice and an endless variety of spinach stalks, edible ferns, crisp leaves and pungent herbs. If the stalks are tough they may have to be lightly blanched before joining the others, but the traditional food of the region is salad.

There is nothing unusual about the contribution of my aunt and myself to this story; foreign vegetables have been coming into Asia for centuries – the Spanish and the Portuguese brought chillies, tomatoes, lady's fingers and the western potato. More recent arrivals include asparagus and some new varieties of mushroom. Our one failure is the artichoke. My aunt and I love them and there should be no reason why we shouldn't grow them in the temperate highlands, but we can't. We've tried and tried but, frustratingly, they just won't take.

I recently had a rare opportunity to see just how much of this traditional 'pick-and-cook' cuisine still survives, thanks to an old friend, Pan Thongchua, who is always up to something interesting. We have a lot in common. At different times we both studied art, I specialized in painting while Pan chose archaeology. While I left for England and the restaurant business, Pan has continued to be part of the creative life of our native land. Today, he teaches Art History and Thai Culture at Thammasat and Silpakorn Universities in Bangkok and at Chiang Mai University in the north. However, it is the extra things that he does which are so fascinating.

He is such an expert on traditional Thai crafts and customs that when there is a special dinner at the Royal Palace, Pan is asked to arrange the decorations and table settings. Everything must be perfect. Sometimes there are teams of craftsmen and craftswomen working from early morning, stitching flowers together so that the King and Queen and guests can walk over a carpet of fresh, scented blossom. On other occasions, the entire evening – food, decorations and costumes – is in a particular period and style.

Pan is an avid student of old documents and records and knows more then anyone about how life was lived in ancient Siam or old Bangkok. So it was no surprise that he was hired to advise the producers of the recent film *Anna and the King*, who were keen that their film should be as authentic as possible. Sadly, the final production was not a critical or commercial success. Thanks to Pan, though, it looked sumptuous.

There is a more serious side to all this. Pan does a lot of work trying to preserve traditional ways that are fast disappearing. Too often, village people are seduced by television into letting ancient festivals and ceremonies die out. Whenever he can, Pan tries to encourage them to preserve the old ways and teach their children to take part before knowledge of how things should be done is lost for ever. He is especially active in the north, where he has a house on the slopes of Doi Inthanon, the highest mountain in Thailand. When I heard that he had managed to save the traditional Kathin ceremony in the nearby village of Yang Luong, I knew I had to find a way to join him.

Kathin comes with the finish of Buddhist Lent when the rainy season is over, roughly the end of October, depending on the moon. Kathin is a religious ceremony where new robes are presented to the monks at the local monastery. The most spectacular Kathin ceremony takes place in Bangkok, when the King and other members of the royal family are rowed, in intricately carved and gilded royal barges, across the Chao Phraya river to offer robes to the monks at Wat Arun, the Temple of the Dawn – famously one of the great spectacles of Asia.

In today's busy world, Kathin is most often a modest affair – worshippers in the big cities usually buy ready-made cloth to take to a temple, whereas in the old days many villages would hold a Chula Kathin ceremony in which the cloth had to be made within a period of twenty-four hours. This generally took place between the midnight preceding the ceremony and the afternoon of the day itself. The whole period was one big party, with eating, drinking, music, dancing, fireworks and sideshows, and many places across Thailand did this. Now, sadly, Chula Kathin has almost universally faded away.

A rare exception was Yang Luong, perhaps because their ceremony was

Kathin Ceremony in Thailand: Royal Barge Procession across the Chao Phraya River to the Temple of the Dawn

slightly different – instead of making robes for the monks, the villagers made a long robe for the giant statue of the Buddha in their surprisingly large, but rather run-down, village temple. And they didn't just sew it within the prescribed time, they picked the cotton, carded and threaded it, then wove and dyed it – quite an achievement. So when he heard that there was talk of giving up this arduous task, Pan leapt into action, talking with the village elders, persuading them to continue, and I decided to join them.

It was late evening when I drove up to Yang Luong and the temple festivities were already beginning. There was the inevitable loud, amplified pop music, and boys swaggering about in their best clothes trying to impress the girls, who had clearly spent hours getting ready for this moment. For once, though, the young ones weren't having all the fun. Pan had cleverly persuaded the elders to forsake the usual beauty contest in favour of a 'best traditional robe' contest.

In this village, while the men farm, the women grow cotton and weave it into some of the most sought-after designs in the north. Inevitably the older a woman is the more time she's had to hone her skills and to collect the best examples of her work. So, for once, parading about in their finery, they and not their daughters or granddaughters were the stars. And how wonderful they were – some in subtle bands of blending colours, others in bold abstract patterns, the rich dyes giving the cotton the sheen of precious silk.

Suddenly there was the sound of drumming and clapping. It was midnight and our Chula Kathin began with a procession of virginal girls dressed in white, who made their way to a fenced-off cotton field to pick the crop for the

A new robe for the Buddha in Wat Yang Luong, northern Thailand

night's labour. They swayed and dipped like temple dancers, pale and beautiful in the light of flickering torches, singing as they worked. When they had collected sufficient cotton, the action split between those who were going to do the work and those who would keep them awake and amused.

First the fluffy cotton was spun into fine threads, but because it was night and there was no sun for drying they could not be dyed, as would usually have been done at this point. That would wait until tomorrow. Then came the weaving on a clattering, foot-operated, wooden loom, its spindle flashing across the weft as the broad length of cloth began to unroll. All around, the music, singing and dancing, and the loud scary explosions of fabulous fireworks, kept everyone awake and happy. By sun-up, it was time for the all-important dyeing. The Buddha and his monks wear only saffron-coloured cloth and the dye is made naturally from juice at the heart of the jackfruit. Transformed into a vibrant orange/yellow, the long strip was stretched over a drying frame to let the sun complete the task.

Now there was a break for lunch, after which the ceremony proper would begin. I was invited to eat in a communal hall, where volunteers had been preparing local specialities since early morning – sticky rice, of course, but for today there was *kanom jin*, a thick white noodle made on feast days, and, for once, plenty of meat – the fatted calf had been slaughtered and would appear in various guises, ground and spiced as *laab* with salad, stewed as curry or just plain barbecued. A pig joined in with another northern curry, *haeng lay*, but the emphasis was still very much on fresh salad and vegetables, the centrepiece a yam salad with tamarind and coriander leaves, young mango leaf, and *makok* (after which Bangkok is named), a cross between an olive and a bitter plum. Sharp-tasting fruits and vegetables like *makok* bring an acid edge to a northern dressing, as lime and lemon are not much used in the region. There was also a salad with small pieces of grilled river fish to bring a salty taste to the mix.

This sort of simple 'pick-and-cook' food is still common in the northern mountainous areas of Southeast Asia, especially in Laos, our neighbour across the Mekong. On a recent visit to the capital, Vientiane, I ate at a food stall opposite the city's main temple, Wat Simuang, and the meal was a memory of a cuisine that is rapidly disappearing in supposedly more sophisticated places. A large lady was busily pounding ingredients in a big earthenware mortar and, even before I smelled the pungent aroma of garlic and limes, I knew that this would be the salad that we Thais call *som tam* and the Lao know as *tam som*, from *tam* to pound and *som* for sour. This is the one Lao dish to have spread far beyond its home territory.

Of course, it has changed during its travels and it is the Bangkok version, as well as the Thai name, that is best known across Southeast Asia and in Thai restaurants around the globe. Thai *som tam* is a mix of grated raw papaya, pounded with long beans, roasted peanuts and dried shrimp, which is then soaked in fish sauce and lime juice with chilli and garlic – a fiery mix that has been blended to satisfy the Thai love of hot food. In Vientiane, however, the original is strikingly different, a subtle mix of raw papaya with little cherry tomatoes, flavoured with liquid extracted from pickled fish to create a sweet, light taste totally different from the Thai sharpness.

This sort of highly flavoured, very liquid salad, sometimes mixed with tiny mud-crabs or other 'meat' elements, is central to Lao cuisine, whether served as a snack with drinks or as part of a main meal. There are many versions of *sam tom* – a dish like *tam tang* mixes cucumber with cherry tomatoes and chillies to give a hot taste that goes well with drinks before a meal or as an accompaniment, not unlike a salsa, to a plate of deep-fried or barbecued chicken – another classic of Lao cooking which is always served with sticky rice, though today what we call fragrant rice, imported from Thailand, is increasingly common. I was happy to stay with the old ways, and after that temple visit all I had was a simple meal of *tam som* with chicken and sticky rice – this was, after all, a 'people's' restaurant.

Back in Yang Luong, and the Kathin ceremony, our meal complete, we set off to join a procession that would carry the cloth into the village, accompanied by music, drumming and song and preceded by two dancers. One was dressed as an exotic bird, turning and fluttering, pursued by another male dancer dressed only in a black waist-cloth, who made violent jumps and spins, hoping in vain to corner the delicate creature, who always managed to break free. At the entrance to the village compound, a group of hunters fired off ancient muskets to scare away any evil spirits who might have slipped in while everyone was distracted.

Then it was into the temple, where we all prostrated ourselves three times before the Buddha, then sat on the floor, legs politely tucked behind us, while the monks, on a raised dais, chanted prayers. Next two young men climbed up some steps behind the statue and unfurled our cloth over the Buddha's left shoulder, letting it fall to his waist. For a moment everyone was quite silent, even the loud pop music momentarily faded, the drumming

ceased, the dancers stilled. One by one, we approached the newly robed statue to offer flowers and incense and prayers for our families and friends and ourselves. I prayed that the village will always make their Kathin cloth and that, from time to time, I might be permitted to come and join them.

Returning to modern Chiang Mai, it was possible to imagine that such things no longer exist. Yet, across much of Southeast Asia the old ways somehow survive, even in the things we eat. While cooking has undoubtedly become more complex, fresh salad dishes are still much in evidence in the cuisines of the nations at the centre of Southeast Asia – Thailand, Laos, Cambodia – the area the French called *Indochine*. You can occasionally see pick-and-cook in the new mega-cities, where busy office workers pluck the wild plants that flourish on the banks of canals, and even on building sites and garage forecourts. While salad is still an essential part of the Southeast Asian meal, in this modern world it is seldom the only thing.

Over the centuries, as people moved from the highland forests to the lowland plains, from river to sea and latterly, from village to town, a simple, largely salad-based cuisine became part of a wider range of dishes. The greatest single change is believed to have come with the introduction of stir-frying from China. This brought about a move from plain, largely fresh, vegetable and fish dishes to sophisticated recipes with meats, sauces and spices that culminated in the elaborate court cuisines prepared for the kings of Siam, Laos and Cambodia. Over time, these filtered down through society to form the basis of today's modern Southeast Asian cooking.

Inevitably, this move away from simplicity had an effect on salads, which were no longer made up only of simple raw or near-raw plants and vegetables, with a dip to add flavour, but became instead more akin to the Western salad, with ingredients being soaked or dressed before being served. The result is the Thai *yam*, and its equivalents in other countries, which at its most extreme is virtually a contradiction in terms, a 'cooked' salad. Well, almost; I think it best to be liberal with definitions where food is concerned.

As regards salads, I like the Burmese approach – one word for salad is *a thoke*, which simply means 'mix', while a word for more complex dishes, usually eaten on their own, *letthoke*, means 'mixed by hand', which is both picturesque and all-inclusive. At one end of the spectrum, plain uncooked plants served with rice and flavoured with nothing more than a dribble of fish sauce or a touch of chilli paste; at the other, a mix of blanched vegetables with cooked meat or fish, and a few spices. The unifying elements are freshness and firmness, cooked on occasions but always swiftly and lightly, for, despite these extremes, our salads still hark back to their 'pick-and-cook' origins.

This may well be one reason why our food has achieved such rapid popularity in the West over the past twenty years. The arrival of Thai food, in particular, coincided with the awakening interest in healthy, low-meat and vegetarian meals. The cuisines of China and India, which preceded Thai cuisine in the West, hardly feature salads. It is possible to spend, as I did, several weeks in China eating fabulous meals but without seeing anything on a table that was not cooked. Similarly, beyond the odd stray lettuce leaf to garnish a plate of tandoori chicken, Indian food also features little that is raw. With such a precedent, it is small wonder that the freshness of Southeast Asian cooking found an appreciative public. Now, with the cuisines of the other Southeast Asian nations beginning to appear in Europe and America, the range of salad dishes is truly astonishing.

Most variations occur because of geography – Burma, Malaysia and Singapore have elements of India in their food, using spices and dairy products unknown elsewhere. The Philippines, because of its long colonial history, has taken much from Spain. Their term for salad, *ensalada*, says it all, though trying to find evidence of that former life is now difficult. While within the modern sprawling capital the walls of the old city – *Intramuros* – still exist, the old Spanish-colonial houses were destroyed in the fighting between the Americans and Japanese at the end of the Second World War.

One such, the reconstructed Casa Manila, is a bold attempt to recapture something of that curious way of life in what became Asia's only Catholic country. The heavy Castilian furniture and porcelain, the inevitable lace and the cut-glass chandeliers, gloomy portraits of saints and martyrs, reveal an alien way of life grafted on to a delicate Oriental culture. While the house is certainly worth a visit, any surviving Spanish influence is more easily experienced in the capital's restaurants. The best I found was the Bistro Remedios in Remedios Circle, the closest Manila gets to an artistic/Bohemian quarter.

At the Bistro it's possible to eat a meal entirely composed of highly individual salads – watercress with egg, or the classic *gising gising*, water spinach stems with chillies and coconut milk. Somehow the parade of modestly sized dishes reminds one of Madrid or Barcelona, which is hardly surprising when one realizes that one is effectively enjoying a leisurely tapas meal. This exactly corresponds to the Southeast Asian habit of friends gathering in a bar at the end of a working day, to drink and nibble tasty salad snacks sent from the kitchen from time to time. Not surprisingly, the Bistro owners run the neighbouring Café Havana, a Cuban tapas bar, which offers entertaining variations on this theme, like the adventurous Hemingway Platos, named for the American author who had a passion for the islands. Literary jokes aside, eating tapas is so entirely in keeping with Asian traditions that this supposedly alien import has been easily absorbed.

If you are in the Remedios area, I strongly recommend a visit to The Library, a nightclub which offers a do-it-yourself cabaret-cum-karaoke compered, or rather bullied along, by a fearsome transvestite comedian. You will need courage, as it is almost guaranteed that any stranger will be hauled up on stage, as I was, and subjected to a more-or-less humiliating interview, then made to sing along to an embarrassing pop song. I have to admit, though, that it was comical to watch other people go through the same ordeal, so I can't complain.

Superficially at least, it does look as if the Spanish connection is being severed. After General MacArthur retook the Philippines and with the continuation of a strong American presence after independence in 1946, there was an inevitable risk that these traditions would be swept away. Yet, given the power of Hollywood and American popular culture, it is remarkable how successful the Filipinos have been in maintaining their own identity.

Something of this can be seen in Manila's main form of public transport, the Jeepney, made locally but clearly adapted from the US Army vehicle, though with flamboyant additions of chrome and paint that aspire to art, or at least pop-art. The front may proclaim that a particular Jeepney is under the protection of Sant Iago or the Blessed Virgin, but the back may well have the less holy if more practical: 'Don't kiss my rear'. Others are clearly personal: 'Don't sleep on the subway darling' or just touching: 'I love you mother'. I saw one where Jesus Christ shared a placard with Donald Duck and yet another which united Juanita Banana and the Teletubbies!

Yet what could have been an out-and-out hamburger culture has actually preserved much of its own ways beneath a surface veneer of total surrender to Uncle Sam. All over the city you see branches of Jollibee, a fast-food restaurant that, at a distance, could be McDonald's, with kids in baseball caps selling standard hamburgers. Closer to, however, one realizes that these self-service cafés manage to retain the superficial pizzazz of an American fast-food outlet while continuing to offer reasonably authentic local cuisine. It's a very Filipino compromise and one which, in an imperfect world, is not to be despised.

Indonesia also manages a deft mix of local and foreign influences. As one of the world's prime tourist sites, one would have expected the island of Bali to have been simply overwhelmed and totally spoiled. That it hasn't is due mainly to the extraordinary capacity of the Balinese to adapt rather than submit, and in the end to make something new which is still uniquely theirs. When I visited the island, I chose to go inland, up into the hills and forests, rather than lie around on the famous Balinese palm-fringed beaches.

I preferred to visit Ubud, famous as the artistic capital of a people that consider all forms of creative activity, whether it be music, dance or painting, essential elements in human life. A small town, almost in the centre of the island, Ubud is crammed with art galleries selling everything from paintings to exquisite batiks. There are open studios and a museum, as well as temple courtyards and community centres, where it is possible to listen to a *gamelan* orchestra or watch a *legong* dance troupe on almost any night of the week. It seems that there is hardly a Balinese who isn't practising some artistic activity or other and, while it is no doubt convenient to earn a few *rupiah* from putting on tourist shows or from selling your paintings in a hotel lobby, there can be no doubting that it is a genuine part of life on the island and only coincidentally a feature of the tourist trade.

Indeed, my first personal experience of this phenomenon came, appropriately enough, in Pasar Ubud, the central market on Jalan Raya, one of the main roads through the town. Most tourists do no more than cast a passing glance at the beautifully composed stacks of fruit and vegetables but, with this book in mind, I was having a good rummage round a stall piled high with tight crisp lettuces and huge sprays of a plant I'd never seen before, when I uncovered some sheets of newspaper stained with very rich colours. I flicked them over and uncovered a set of beautiful close-up portraits of Balinese men and women in traditional headdresses in a style that seemed to bring

An intricately decorated Hindu temple, evidence of the rich ethnic mix that is modern Singapore

together delicate Oriental stylization with the power of Western realism. As I stood admiring the little pictures I was suddenly aware of being watched – by the stall-holder, who was also the artist, clearly nervous about my reaction to his work. I quickly reassured him and even offered to buy some of them. I have them before me as I write.

This happy mix of East and West, the story of modern Balinese culture, has always been a two-way traffic. In 1597, when the first European visitor, the Dutch captain Cornelius de Houtman, tried to sail away, his crew mutinied, unwilling to be expelled from paradise. Over the succeeding centuries the island played host to a gaggle of romantic drifters in search of something that was missing from wherever they came. Inevitably, among them were a good many artists, but it was a German painter, Walter Spies, who had most effect on local culture. His story would make a fascinating, if ultimately tragic, film.

Arriving on the island after the First World War, Spies devoted himself to encouraging village music and dance, but it was his own romantic paintings of Bali and the Balinese that provoked a cultural revolution when local artists began to apply such Western techniques as perspective and chiaroscuro to traditional scenes. This liberated Balinese art from a rigid tradition and spurred a creative outpouring that can be seen in Ubud's Necker Museum, where room after room of brilliantly coloured canvases reveal the scale of what one man unleashed. Sadly, Spies was arrested by the Dutch colonial authorities at the outbreak of the Second World War and died when the prison ship taking him away from the place he had loved was sunk. He lives on today, his memory honoured by the descendants of those he had known, a symbol of the openness of the Balinese to ideas from whatever source.

This spirit lives on today in a building not far from the museum – Ari's Warung on Ubud Main Road. Ari's began as a small café about 15 years ago, when the owners of the land decided to built an extension to their home where they could sell fruit juice and rice dishes to passers-by. Ari's quickly became popular with visitors, as did the owner, who became something of a local legend for a succession of Western girlfriends whose influence clearly helped transform a small local snack bar into the world-class restaurant it is today. Much of the credit, though, must clearly go to French/American chef Chris Salans, who has taken the original Balinese dishes and transformed them, much as Walter Spies redirected Balinese art. With space for 140 diners, either in the teak-lined room downstairs or on the open rooftop terrace, Ari's is clearly a major institution in Ubud's culinary scene, and several salads in this book draw on the delicious originals I enjoyed there.

In a way, I had expected Indonesian and Philippine food to reflect the foreign influences that have been such a feature of their history, but I also assumed that Vietnam would be much more insular. It is, after all, usual for books on the country to highlight the fact that its people are not really Southeast Asian at all, but much more recent immigrants from southern China – late arrivals in the region, their whole culture, including their food, just a faint echo of that of the Celestial Empire. Yet, if so, how to explain the fact that the Vietnamese are gargantuan salad eaters, a thing unthinkable in mainland China? In fact, the Vietnamese could claim the title of Asia's greatest salad eaters, as you can see in any restaurant or on any food-stall across the country, but especially in what used to be the southern capital and is still the main business centre for the country.

As the central district of the newly named Ho Chi Minh City is still called Saigon, nothing much has changed there, though the new skyscraper hotels and luxury condos tell a different story. Like Laos, Vietnam seems to relish the contradictions that flourish in the gaps left where its communist past meets a confused capitalist present. On a sidewalk stall in Cholon, the old Chinese quarter, a T-shirt sports the familiar goatee-bearded face of Uncle Ho, the ascetic socialist thinker who led the North to freedom from the French but died before his dream of a unified independent Vietnam could be realized. Even when president of North Vietnam, Ho Chi Minh continued to live a monk-like existence in a modest wooden house in the grounds of the former residence of the French Governor in Hanoi. Now he's a T-shirt.

Hanging beside him was a paper suit for Chinese worshippers to burn in honour of their ancestors. You can watch families praying as they throw these paper gifts into temple ovens. You can see paper money, paper cars, even paper watches and paper passports, anything that might please or be useful in the afterlife. Nothing is missing – on the paper breast pocket of the paper suit was a little paper label, that unmistakable red-and-white box with the familiar words 'Tommy Hilfiger'. Oh yes, America's consumer culture has hit Uncle Ho's city in a big way.

Of course, just outside Saigon, in the countryside, the old Vietnam goes on, the only signs of the years of war and political oppression being the huge Soviet-style war-memorials that dominate the landscape. Far more moving are the plain rectangular concrete blocks that one sees in every field. They could be eerily modern abstract sculptures, but turn out to be the graves of the peasant-farmers who worked the land and who refuse to be separated from it even in death. The lush green of the Vietnamese countryside, so well watered by river and rain, makes a vivid backdrop to these brilliant white blocks that almost shine in the intense sunlight.

Painting bought in the vegetable market, Ubud, central Bali

This is particularly noticeable in the South, where the fields are watered by the many outlets of the Mekong and other rivers. Here is a world of orchards so verdant they look like jungle enclaves. This richness may explain why every Vietnamese meal has at its heart a great clump of leaves and stems and salad vegetables, which come unbidden to the table as if they – and not the rice – were the staple of the meal, which in a way they are.

One day, in a small village restaurant I made a note of what was brought out and it really was astonishing. At the very least there was a whole head of lettuce, split up, a big pile of white cabbage leaves, substantial bunches of mint, coriander and spring onions, a whole cucumber, peeled and cut into thick sticks, a handful of beansprouts, a smaller bunch of chives and a small bunch of darker leaves with a purple tinge and tasting of lemon/mint, a fairly strong flavour to be used sparingly. This I later learned was most likely perilla or sisho leaf (tia to), which can sometimes be found in Japanese food stores. On top of all this, were peeled and diced sour apple and star fruit.

As I say, this just comes and basically you do what you will with it, though there is a classic starter which involves a stack of rice sheets which are used as the base on which a selection of the leaves, herbs and fruit is piled, followed by some richly flavoured grilled meat and a dribble of sauce. The whole thing is then rolled up and eaten like a giant spring roll. This basic salad can be a meal in itself and will clearly vary according to the season and the inclinations of the chef, but something like it is always served.

Which, when you think about it, is quite odd. After all, the Vietnamese were originally from China – Nam Viet was a Chinese term for all lands to the south of the Celestial Empire, and for centuries the country was administered from Peking. But the Chinese don't much care for raw food, so how come this complete reversal so close to hand? Some credit the French with the phenomenon, using as evidence the way the Vietnamese, like the Laotians and the Cambodians, have continued to bake baguette and make pâté long after they kicked out their former masters. In the same way, so the theory goes, the Vietnamese have taken to the French salad course. What this doesn't explain is why, in Vietnam, this basic salad is not dressed or eaten as a special course, and why it is even used almost like a condiment, with leaves and herbs being stirred into soups and noodle dishes. No, there is something just too flamboyant about this ever-present greenery for it to be compared to the side dish of lettuce and vinaigrette you often get in France.

You will see what I mean if, at serious risk to your life, you launch yourself across the multi-lane intersection that engulfs the Tran Nguyen Hai statue to arrive (it is to be hoped) at Saigon's Ban Thanh market. The cluster of stalls in the food section at the back of the main hall are so close to the huge mounds of fresh produce, they are in the perfect position to offer their customers salad heaven. I picked a stall called Bun Mam, which the owner explained was the name of their main dish – which, of course, I then ordered. Bun are the thin vermicelli or glass noodles, mam means water or liquid, but in culinary terms refers to a sauce, as in nuoc mam, the basic fish sauce. At this particular stall the sauce was mam nem, similar but made with anchovies rather than ordinary fish and therefore more pungent. This strong taste is balanced by the addition of fresh sweet pineapple and this sauce is served in a little dish with the noodles in another, along with a bowl of rich broth containing the meat of your choice – beef, chicken, shrimp, whatever – and of course a sensational clump of salad as described above.

After that its pretty much up to you how you tackle the feast – slurp your soup and swallow your noodles and salad separately, or roll them up with some sauce, or if you prefer, drop salad and sauce and noodles into the soup. No one cares, and you will always get more salad should you need any, which I doubt. In South Vietnam noodles – pho – are usually eaten for breakfast, but this place was unusual in having a reputation that kept it going all day. It all comes down to the constantly evolving stock used for the soup. I suspect the one they were serving had been on the go since the last Vietnamese Emperor, Bo Dai, sat on the jade throne, which is no doubt why it was so delicious.

If you don't have salad aversion after a dish like that you could always have spring rolls, which also come with a greenhouse full of leaves. It was all so amazingly healthy, and a fitting climax to my search for the best salads in the region. From the simple pleasures of pick-and-cook in the north of Thailand and Laos, to the complex multicultural dishes of Indonesia and the Philippines, the salads of Southeast Asia are history and culture on a plate. I have enjoyed tracking them down. I hope you will enjoy eating them and sharing something of the places and peoples that created them.

Opposite: Floating Market, the Mekong Delta, southern Vietnam

before you begin

The average Western kitchen should have all the equipment necessary for these recipes, though it would be an advantage to have a large mortar and pestle. For preparation and serving, you'll need at least one large and one small bowl and a largish serving platter. The amounts given here will produce dishes sufficient for a light snack for two people if eaten on their own, or enough for four if part of a larger meal with other dishes. Any unusual techniques are explained with the ingredients to which they relate, either as part of a recipe or, if they recur frequently, then below in the section called Cooking Techniques.

ingredients

I have not included here ingredients familiar in the West such as onions, unless there was something unusual about our use of them, nor have I included Eastern ingredients, such as beansprouts, that are now common-place around the world. It is best to remember that vegetables in Asia tend to be smaller than those in Europe or America, so try not to select giant bulbous specimens when shopping for these recipes. As a general principle, everything should be cut into bite-sized pieces (as we seldom use knives at table) and always under- rather than over-cook.

basic salads

In the main, there are two types of salad in this book: those in which the principal ingredients are tossed or covered in a sauce and those in which the salad is served on the side. These latter are again divided in two: those with crisp or 'hard' ingredients and those with 'soft' ingredients. As they frequently recur, it will be easier if I describe them here rather than repeat the same recipe over and over again.

Crisp salad

As the name implies, this consists of firm or hard crunchy vegetables and leaves that can stand up to a strong, powerfully flavoured dip or other highly spiced mixture. The firm leaves can be used as a scoop or a wrap to convey the mixture to the mouth, where it will counterbalance the heat and add a crunchy texture. A typical crisp salad might contain iceberg lettuce leaves, white cabbage, chopped long bean, tomato and cucumber, together with grated or finely diced vegetables, such as carrots.

Mixed seasonal salad

This is the 'soft' salad. The recipes provide a range of dressings, where I've simply specified 'mixed seasonal salad' the choice of fresh ingredients is up to you, just find the freshest available. The variety is staggering, there are now almost too many lettuces: escarole, radicchio, Cos, frisée, lamb's lettuce, baby butter lettuce; along with other greens: endive, baby spinach, watercress, baby sorrel, Swiss chard, and once unusual leaves like rocket, mustard greens and kale. Other possible candidates include fresh herbs, such as flowering chives and chervil, not to mention edible flowers like nasturtiums and courgette flowers, and a range of specialist vegetables like miniature yellow pear tomatoes and tiny bell peppers. The shopping is almost as much fun as the eating.

Opposite: Traditional kitchen, Thailand

fresh ingredients

Aubergine (eggplant)

Four varieties of aubergine are used in Southeast Asian cuisine, two soft and two hard. The soft aubergines are the large purple/black aubergine familiar in the West and the long, thin pink-skinned aubergine. The hard ones are the small, round green aubergine, about 2.5cm (1in) in diameter, and the pea aubergine, also green and rather like an inflated garden pea. These last two will only be available in specialist Oriental stores.

Bamboo shoot

The 'shoot' is the first soft stage of the bamboo when it appears out of the ground, before it hardens into the cane known in the West. The shoot has to be stripped of its needle-sharp hairs and boiled to remove the bitter, poisonous acid. Don't worry, even in Asia they are bought ready-prepared by experts and in the West they are always bought canned. They can be divided into 'spring' shoots and 'winter' shoots, the latter considered the most tender and sweet. Unfortunately the cans seldom indicate which variety is contained. Canned in brine, they are yellowish in colour and may be kept in water in a sealed container in a refrigerator for several days.

Banana flower (banana blossom, banana heart)

The banana flower will only be available in specialist, generally Chinese, shops and then only rarely. It is a dramatic, large purple/red closed flower not unlike an outsize unopened tulip. It is best treated as a vegetable not dissimilar to fennel. Prepare the flower by removing all layers of purple petals down to the young pale pink layer. Quarter the remaining flower lengthwise, place in a pan of boiling water and simmer for 15 minutes. Drain, leave to cool and then cut each quarter at an angle into thin slices.

Basil

Sweet basil (the variety most commonly found in Europe) has shiny green leaves edged with purple, and a smell tinged with cinnamon and cloves. It is cooked at the last minute or used fresh as a garnish. Holy, or Thai, basil has narrower, slightly hairy leaves, a stronger taste; it must be cooked.

Bitter melon (bitter gourd, spiny bitter gourd, karela, kantola)

This is an immature baby melon, pear-shaped with a green warty skin. The flavour has been described as cucumber with the bitterness of chicory leaves. It is best eaten when young and its 'quinine' bitterness is freshest. Scrape away the coarsest part of the skin, split it open and remove the inner seeds and the soft pith that surrounds them, then slice according to the recipe.

Calamansi, see Lime

Chilli

Three varieties are used in this book: small red or green chillies about 2.5cm (1in) long and pretty hot; medium chillies, red or green, finger length, about 7.5cm (3in) long and less hot: large dried red chillies about 7.5cm (3in) long and with medium heat.

Chinese celery (illustrated opposite)

This is similar to Western celery but has looser stems with a smaller diameter and a much stronger flavour, which means some adjustment if you substitute another variety. Choose those with the fattest and whitest stalks, as these will be the most tender. Chop them more finely than you would with Western celery as they can be stringy.

Chinese kale

Its characteristic little white flowers distinguish Chinese kale from other forms of Chinese cabbage. Choose those with flowers in bud not bloom, and with thicker stems. The leaves are tougher and have a taste stronger than cabbage, while the stems are more succulent.

Coriander

Closely resembling Italian or flat-leaf parsley, coriander leaves are used as a garnish, while the tiny roots and/or stalks are much used, crushed, as a cooking ingredient. Roots and stalks can be frozen.

Eggplant, see Aubergine

Galangal

This creamy-white rhizome is slightly harder than ginger (see below); it is used in the same way but has a more lemony flavour.

Ginger

Knobbly, golden-beige 'fingers' of fresh ginger are now readily available, but are often old and musty. Try to get young 'roots' (ginger is actually a rhizome) which are pinker in colour. Well wrapped, these can keep for up to 2 weeks in a refrigerator. They also freeze well and can be grated while frozen.

Kaffir lime, see Lime

Lemon grass

This important herb is sold as long lemony-scented blades, always with the leaves chopped off. Try to buy pale-green, near-white, bulbous stalks, roughly 23cm (9in) long. If old, you will need to peel away the hard outer leaves down to the tender centre. When cooked, lemon grass imparts a fresh citrus taste with a touch of ginger, but without the bitter acidity of lemon or lime. Rings of chopped lemon grass may be frozen and used direct from the deep-freeze.

Lime

Little green limes are the most common citrus flavouring in Southeast Asian cooking – you will need a lot for these recipes. Lemons can be substituted at a pinch. Kaffir lime is not used for its juice, of which there is virtually none, but for its skin or zest, which has a strong citrus punch, or its leaves, which add tang when cooked. The Philippines has a particularly strong orangey lime, the calamansi, which appears to be unavailable elsewhere but which I mention in that chapter.

Long bean

At up to a metre (3 feet) in length, the aptly named long bean resembles a wildly overgrown string bean (which can be used as a substitute). The long bean, however, is crunchier and cooks faster. Choose darker beans with small bean seeds inside the pods.

Lotus stem (lotus root)

This rhizome, often served as a vegetable, looks like a string of bulbous sausages and needs careful preparation. It is easier to buy them canned. Slightly sweet, with a crunchy texture, the canned ones lose a little of this but are perfectly acceptable.

Mooli, see White radish

Morning glory (water spinach)

With a slight flavour of Western spinach, the long jointed stems of this water vegetable remain firm when cooked, while the arrow-shaped leaves quickly go limp. The leaves quickly turn yellow and go bad if not used promptly.

Mushroom

Dried fungus mushrooms (cloud ears): these are the most common Asian mushroom; easily available, they are usually black but there is a white variety. Usually bought in 60g (2oz) packets, they should be soaked at room temperature until soft (20 – 30 minutes), then checked to see that no sandy grit remains. The smaller they are the better. Readily available and suitable Western varieties include the champignon or button mushroom, the large flat parasol mushroom and the straw mushroom, which is slightly more pointed than the button mushroom, as well as the oyster or pleurotte mushroom.

Papaya (pawpaw)

This large, green gourd-like fruit with soft yellow-orange flesh is eaten like melon. When unripe and still green, the hard flesh is grated and used as a vegetable.

Pomelo

Sometimes known as shaddock, the pomelo is not unlike a large hard grapefruit (a reasonable substitute), but with a much thicker rind and less juicy flesh which is pink or greeny white.

Market at Hoi An, central Vietnam

Rice, sticky or glutinous

Nearly always served with northern Thai or Lao food, this is a broad short-grain rice, mostly white but sometimes brown, even black. When cooked, it is thick and slightly porridgy and can be rolled into a ball and used as a scoop for other food. Sadly, it cannot be cooked in an electric rice-steamer.

To cook 450g (1lb) sticky rice, soak in just enough water to cover for at least 3 hours, preferably overnight. Drain and rinse thoroughly. Line the perforated part of a steamer with a double thickness of muslin or cheesecloth and turn the rice into it. Bring water at the bottom of the steamer to the boil and steam the rice over a moderate heat for 30 minutes.

Turmeric

Brown and flaky without, bright orange-yellow within, this rhizome adds a warm, spicy taste but is used mostly dried and ground to add colour. Fresh turmeric is now more easily available in the West, but only buy small amounts. Treat fresh turmeric like ginger: cut off a small section, peel it and chop or pound it according to the instructions in the recipe.

Water spinach, see Morning glory

White radish (mooli, daikon)

This long, large white root vegetable, with a cool sharpness when raw, is a bit like turnip when cooked. It is often found among Japanese produce, where it will be called daikon.

cooking techniques

Boiling poultry

We have a way of cooking chicken or duck breast that ensures they are neither tough nor overcooked. Place the breast in a pan, just cover with cold water, bring to the boil then remove from the heat. Cover with the pan lid and leave in the boiled water for 10 minutes, until just cooked through.

Crisp-frying

To add flavour and a crunchy texture to a dish, some ingredients – like dried shrimps, chopped garlic and shallots, and shredded lime leaf – can be fried in hot oil until they are crisp. To shred the lime leaves, pile them on top of one another, roll them into 'cigarettes' and cut these across in very thin slices, which will produce fine slivers of leaf.

Dry-frying

Again to add flavour and a crunchy texture to a dish, ingredients like grated coconut, uncooked rice grains, sesame seeds (white or black), sunflower seeds, etc., are placed in a frying pan without oil and heated until they darken and release their aroma – sesame seeds will jump around as they warm up.

Grinding or powdering

Dry-fried ingredients are sometimes ground to a powder in a mortar. This will impart the same flavour but produce a different, smoother texture in a dish. Dried shrimps can be ground to a fine white powder, but this preparation can also be bought ready-ground in packets.

ready-prepared ingredients

Beancurd (tofu)

Blocks of white fresh beancurd are sold in plastic trays, in a little of their own milky liquid, usually divided into nine cubes. They are best used the day of purchase, but may be kept for up to 3 days in a refrigerator provided the liquid is poured away each day and replaced with fresh water. Cubes of deep-fried beancurd are usually available in Chinese stores, but deep-frying your own fresh beancurd until it is golden brown produces something so superior I strongly recommend making the extra effort involved.

Chilli oil

One method of making this involves fresh garlic and shallots and dried chillies being first grilled, pounded to a paste and then stir-fried in oil to give it a powerful, hot flavour. In another, the ingredients are fried in oil until crisp, then pounded and stir-fried. You can make it yourself, but there is little point; simply buy it ready-made in bottles. Each country has its own version, but there is little difference between them. You will only need quite small amounts, but it will keep, well sealed, in a refrigerator for at least a year.

Chilli powder

This red powder made by grinding small dried red chillies is sold in jars, cans, packets or cardboard containers.

Coconut milk, cream

Buy this in cans: when it has settled the thin liquid at the top of the can is coconut milk; stirred or shaken, so that it mixes with the thicker matter below, it becomes coconut cream – it's as simple as that!

Dried shrimp

These tiny sun-dried shrimp sold loose or in jars or plastic bags will keep for a long time. They are not meant to be reconstituted by soaking in water, but for use as a flavouring. Chose those that are not too pink or salty. See also Shrimp Paste below.

Fermented anchovy sauce

Buy this bottled. Well sealed in a refrigerator, it will keep for ages.

Fish sauce

The 'salt' of Southeast Asia, this liquid extracted from fermented fish is the principal savoury taste in nearly all the recipes in this book. The best is young, has a light whisky colour and a refreshingly salty taste; the worst is old, dark and bitter. The easiest to find are those from Thailand (*nam pla*) or Vietnam (*nuoc mam*). The amount of fish sauce in a dish is clearly a matter of taste. I have prescribed modest quantities, so taste and add more if you wish. Strict vegetarians, who do not eat fish, should substitute light soy sauce, bearing in mind that it is less salty so more will be needed.

Noodles

There are 6 varieties of noodle commonly used in Southeast Asia, but you will only need 3 for the recipes in this book:
Egg noodles – yellow, thin, spaghetti-like, they come in 'nests' which need to be shaken loose before or during cooking. They are available fresh or dried.
Clear vermicelli (glass or cellophane noodles) – very thin, wiry, translucent soya bean noodles, these are only available dried.
Rice noodles (sometimes called rice river noodles or rice sticks) – broad, flat, white rice flour noodles. Although usually bought fresh in rather sticky strands that have to be prised apart before cooking, they are also available dried.

Most dried noodles need to be soaked in cold water for 20 minutes, this will double the weight, after which they should be drained, then dunked in boiling water for 2 to 3 seconds, which is sufficient to cook them.

Oil, vegetable, olive, sesame, nut

As a general rule, Southeast Asian cookery demands a neutral-flavoured vegetable oil both for cooking or as an ingredient. Flavours are often added – by frying garlic or shallots in the oil at the beginning of the cooking process. There are occasional exceptions: some Chinese-based dishes require sesame oil for its rich flavour, some dishes come from territories that produce a particularly flavourful nut oil (generally peanut, which is most commonly sold here as 'groundnut oil'), which colours the dish and which can be reproduced by using pure nut oil from a health food supplier, though it is expensive. Uniquely for Asia, The Philippines, under the heavy influence of Spain, has taken to using olive oil for some of its dishes, especially salads. For all other countries in the region, however, olive and other distinctively flavoured oils, should be strictly avoided.

Palm sugar

Sold in compressed cakes which keep well, the best palm sugar is soft and brown and has a rich toffee-like aroma. It is essential if you want the full caramel taste of some Southeast Asian dishes. Dark Demerara sugar is a possible, but poor, substitute.

Pickled or fermented fish

Pieces of fish are salted and preserved to produce a rich, very salty, smelly liquid. You will need a jar of it – nationality doesn't matter and it keeps for ages. Boil a little before use to kill off any impurities.

Shrimp paste

This dark purple paste has a formidable smell that disappears on cooking and adds a rich pungent taste to any dish. Store in a tightly sealed jar or risk a malodorous kitchen. See also Dried Shrimp above.

Soy sauce

Light soy sauce is light-coloured, almost clear, with a delicately salty taste. Dark soy sauce is thicker and stronger and used mainly to add colour to a dish.

Spring roll sheets

These paper-thin pastry wrappers may be bought ready-made in packets.

Tamarind (illustrated opposite)

The pulp extracted from the pods of the tamarind tree is used to impart a pungent, sour, lemony flavour. Buy it in compressed blocks. Most recipes call for it to be dissolved in water to make 'tamarind water' or 'tamarind liquid'. Place a lump of tamarind, roughly equivalent to a heaped tablespoon, in warm water and knead it until the water is deep brown and all the flavour has been extracted. Discard the mashed tamarind.

Vinegar, rice, white

While rice vinegar would be authentic, usually any plain light white wine vinegar will do.

'So there it is, a perfect, easy and very cheap meal – rice, spice and an endless variety of spinach stalks, edible ferns, crisp leaves and pungent herbs. If the stalks are tough they may have to be lightly blanched before joining the others, but basically the traditional food of the region is salad.'

Painting of a devotee offering food to a monk, dating back to the late eighteenth or early nineteenth century, on the walls of an island temple in the Chao Phraya river in Nonthaburi, Thailand

pomelo and grilled prawn salad

yam somo

We only make this salad if we've bought a sour pomelo that isn't sweet enough to eat as a fruit; so a grapefruit makes a fair substitute.

6 large lettuce leaves

8 large king prawns

250g (9oz) pomelo segments, broken into small pieces

for the dressing

4 small red shallots

3 garlic cloves

4 small red chillies

1 tablespoon fish sauce

1 teaspoon palm sugar

2 tablespoons coconut cream

1 heaped tablespoon dry-fried coconut (see page 23)

1 heaped tablespoon ground dried shrimp (see page 23)

1 Arrange the lettuce leaves on a serving platter and set aside.

2 Preheat the grill to hot and grill the prawns in their shells until they just change colour. When cool enough to handle, peel and devein them. Place the prawns and pomelo segments in a bowl and set aside.

3 Prepare the dressing: wrap the shallots, garlic and chillies in foil and grill the parcel for 1 minute on each side. Then remove the foil, place the contents in a mortar and pound to a paste. Add the fish sauce, sugar and coconut cream and stir well. Pour the dressing over the salad and mix well.

4 Just before serving, stir the coconut and ground shrimp into the salad, turn out on to the serving platter with the lettuce leaves and serve at once.

Massive limestone outcrops rise out of the sea at Phangnga Bay near Phuket

tuna salad yam tuna

I decided to make this with canned rather than fresh tuna, as a storecupboard stand-by. You could use this, without lettuce, as a sandwich filling.

6 large lettuce leaves

150g (5oz) canned tuna in oil, well drained

5 small red shallots, thinly sliced

2 heaped teaspoons grated ginger

1 young lemon grass stalk, thinly sliced into rounds

2 spring onions, roughly sliced

3 small red chillies, finely chopped

1 tablespoon fish sauce

1 level teaspoon sugar

1 tablespoon lime juice

1 Arrange the lettuce leaves on a serving platter and set aside.

2 Flake the tuna into a bowl. Add all the remaining ingredients and stir well.

3 Turn out on to the platter with the lettuce and serve.

grilled chicken salad
gai yang nam tok

Possibly the most famous food area in Bangkok is Lang Suan, with dozens of restaurants and food stalls clustered in the streets and alleyways surrounding the road of that name. I am fortunate in that it can easily be reached on foot by navigating the maze of dusty lanes between the surviving wooden shacks at the back of my apartment block in the centre of town. I'd often heard older people talk about a great restaurant just called the Lang Suan, but I'd never been able to track it down, until one night I was out with some friends and we drifted into one of these passages that I'd previously written off as a cul-de-sac. It was a dead end, but at the bottom was a scruffy little 'shop-house' packed with people and, yes, it was the famous Lang Suan Restaurant. Clearly it wasn't going to win any prizes in the decoration and cleanliness stakes, but the food was good enough to keep everyone's mind off such shortcomings. Everything we ate had that touch of brilliance about it, especially this grilled chicken salad.

1 skinless chicken breast fillet
mixed seasonal salad
20 mint leaves

for the marinade
1 tablespoon fish sauce
2 level teaspoons finely chopped garlic
1 heaped teaspoon finely chopped coriander
½ teaspoon ground black pepper
1 heaped teaspoon sugar
½ teaspoon ground turmeric

for the dressing
2 tablespoons fish sauce
2 tablespoons lime juice
2 level teaspoons sugar
3 small red shallots, thinly sliced
½ teaspoon chilli powder
1 level tablespoon ground dry-fried rice (see page 23)

1 Mix all the marinade ingredients in a bowl, add the chicken and leave to marinate for about 1 hour.

2 In another bowl, prepare the dressing: mix the fish sauce, lime juice and sugar, stir well, then add the shallots and chilli powder, mix and set aside.

3 Preheat a moderate to hot grill. Arrange the mixed salad and the mint leaves on a serving platter and set aside.

4 Remove the chicken from the marinade and grill until cooked through, about 5 minutes on each side. Then, when it is cool enough to handle, thinly slice it at an angle.

5 Place the chicken slices in the bowl with the dressing and mix well.

6 Just before serving, stir in the ground dry-fried rice, turn out on to the salad platter and serve.

egg noodle salad yam ba mee

2 nests of dried *ba mee* (egg noodles, see page 24)

60g (2oz) pork fillet

60g (2oz) skinless chicken breast fillet

60g (2oz) raw prawns

6 large lettuce leaves

1 onion, halved and then thinly sliced

10 cherry tomatoes, halved

2 celery stalks, thinly sliced

1 small carrot, cut into thin matchsticks

2 spring onions, roughly chopped

1 level tablespoon finely chopped mint leaves

for the dressing

4 garlic cloves

3 small red shallots

2 dry chillies

2 tablespoons fish sauce

2 tablespoons lime juice

2 level teaspoons sugar

2 heaped tablespoons ground roast peanuts

1 Bring a pan of water to the boil, add the noodles and simmer until they soften and separate. Remove, drain, and hold under cold running water to stop the cooking process. The noodles should be just al dente, i.e. tender but still firm. Drain well again and set aside.

2 Place the pork in a pan, cover with water, bring to the boil and simmer until cooked through, about 3 minutes. Remove and set aside. Place the chicken in the boiling water and simmer until cooked through, about 4 – 5 minutes. Remove and set aside. Briefly dip the prawns in the boiling water, until they just change colour. Remove and set aside.

3 Make the dressing: preheat a hot grill. Wrap the garlic, shallot and chillies in foil and grill the parcel for 1 minute on each side. Remove the foil, place the contents in a mortar and pound to a paste. Add the fish sauce, lime juice and sugar, and stir until it dissolves. Set aside.

4 Thinly slice the pork at an angle, then cut the slices into thin strips and place in a bowl. Tear the chicken into small pieces and add to the bowl. Peel and devein the prawns (leaving their tails on if you prefer), and place in the bowl. Add the noodles and the remaining ingredients with the dressing and mix well.

5 Just before serving, add the ground peanuts. Stir, turn out on a plate and serve.

'... when fishermen still offered fresh-caught fish to be grilled on an open fire on the sands.'

squid salad laab pla muk

Twenty years ago I arrived on the island of Phuket just as they were ceremonially opening the new international airport that would transform the island into one of the world's major tourist destinations. I can claim to have had one of the last holidays when it was possible to sleep in a wooden beach hut and when fishermen still offered fresh-caught fish to be grilled on an open fire on the sands. Today, it's Miami, with a line of skyscraper hotels running right round the shore. Recently, I was walking along Patong beach, Mecca for charter-flight tours, feeling a bit gloomy, when I spotted a beachside restaurant, grabbed a chair and ordered squid salad and a glass of Mekong whiskey. Facing out to sea, with all the new buildings behind me, things looked pretty much as they had all those years ago. The spicy salad was as good as ever, the whiskey very relaxing and I began to take a more positive view of things. After all, things aren't that bad. Thousands now enjoy something previously reserved for the fortunate few. So best to eat and drink and stop moaning.

225g (8oz) fresh squid, cleaned and roughly chopped
1 young lemon grass stalk, thinly sliced
1 heaped teaspoon finely chopped galangal
4 small red shallots, thinly sliced
3 spring onions, roughly chopped
4 small red chillies, finely chopped
1 heaped tablespoon roughly chopped coriander
1 tablespoon fish sauce
2 level teaspoons sugar
2 tablespoons lime juice
1 heaped tablespoon ground dry-fried rice (see page 23)
crisp salad, to serve

1 Place 2 tablespoons of water in a pan. Add the squid and bring to a simmer. Add all the remaining ingredients except the rice and salad, stir well and simmer for 1 minute.

2 Remove from the heat, stir in the rice, turn out on a serving plate and serve accompanied by the crisp salad.

sweetcorn salad yam kowpohd

100g (4oz) pork fillet

225g (8oz) boiled sweetcorn segments

1 carrot, sliced into thin matchsticks

1 heaped tablespoon crisp-fried shallots (see page 23)

1 heaped tablespoon crisp-fried garlic (see page 23)

1 heaped tablespoon crisp-fried kaffir lime leaf (see page 23)

for the dressing

3 garlic cloves, finely chopped

3 small red chillies, finely chopped

2 tablespoons fish sauce

1 heaped teaspoon sugar

2 tablespoons lemon juice

1 Bring a pan of just enough water to cover the pork to the boil. Add the pork and boil until just cooked through, about 3 minutes. When cool enough to handle, remove and cut across the grain into thin strips.

2 Put the pork in a bowl with all the remaining salad ingredients and set aside.

3 In another bowl, mix all the dressing ingredients together well. Pour over the salad, toss and serve.

bitter melon salad yam malat

1 skinless chicken breast fillet
1 large green bitter melon

for the dressing
5 shallots
4 garlic cloves
1 large dry chilli, roughly chopped
2 tablespoons lime juice
2 tablespoons fish sauce
2 level teaspoons sugar
2 tablespoons coconut cream
1 heaped tablespoon dry-fried sesame seeds (see page 23)

1 Bring a pan of water to the boil, add the chicken and simmer until just cooked through, about 10 minutes. When cool enough to handle, remove and, using the fingers, shred into a bowl.

2 Halve the bitter melon lengthwise, then quarter. Remove the seeds, then slice the melon into 1cm (½in) pieces. Dip the bitter melon pieces into the boiling water and briefly blanch, ensuring that they remain al dente. Drain well, place in the bowl with the chicken and set aside.

3 Prepare the dressing: preheat a hot grill. Wrap the shallots, garlic and chillies in foil and grill the parcel for 1 minute on each side. Remove the flavourings from the foil, place in a mortar and pound to a paste. Stir in the lime juice, fish sauce and sugar, and stir until the sugar dissolves.

4 Pour the dressing over the chicken and bitter melon. Stir well.

5 Just before serving, stir in the coconut cream and sesame seeds.

white fungus mushroom salad
yam het hoo noo kaow

This mushroom is from the same family as the more common black fungus mushroom found in all Chinese stores. In truth, the white ones are chosen only for their appearance; if reasonably large, they resemble a flower. If you can't find them, use the black variety. If you want this dish to look good, leave the prawns whole; but if you want to improve the taste, chop them up.

60g (2oz) minced pork
60g (2oz) dried white fungus mushrooms, soaked as described page 22
8 large peeled cooked prawns, whole or chopped (see above)
1 carrot, cut into thin matchsticks
85g (3oz) Chinese celery, cut into thin matchsticks
60g (2oz) roast cashew nuts

for the dressing
2 tablespoons fish sauce
2 tablespoons lime juice
2 level teaspoons sugar
3 small red or green chillies, finely chopped
3 garlic cloves, finely chopped
2 small red shallots, thinly sliced

1 Make the dressing: mix all the ingredients in a bowl and set aside.

2 Put 2 tablespoons of water in a pan, add the pork and heat to a simmer until cooked through, about 2 – 3 minutes. Stir in the prawns, followed by the drained and roughly chopped mushrooms. Turn out into another bowl.

3 Stir in the carrot and celery, then add the dressing and mix well. Just before serving, stir in the cashew nuts.

oyster salad
yam hoy nang rom

mixed seasonal salad
1 young lemon grass stalk, thinly sliced
4 small red shallots, thinly sliced
1 level tablespoon ginger that has been cut into thin strips
3 garlic cloves, thinly sliced
3 small red chilli, finely chopped
2 tablespoons fish sauce
2 teaspoons palm sugar
4 tablespoons lemon juice
1 dozen fresh oysters, off the shell
10 mint leaves, roughly chopped, to garnish

1 Arrange the salad on a serving platter and set aside.

2 Put all the remaining ingredients except the oysters and mint in a bowl, mix well and set aside.

3 Bring a pan of water to the boil, momentarily dip the oysters in the water, drain well and place in the bowl with the salad.

4 Stir well, turn out on to the platter with the salad and serve.

Opposite: Fishermen, Songkhla Harbour, southern Thailand.

roast duck salad yam pet yang

mixed seasonal salad

1 duck breast fillet

60g (2oz) small fresh pineapple segments

60g (2oz) cucumber, halved lengthwise, deseeded, then cut across
into crescents

1 large tomato, cut into small cubes

1 onion, halved and thinly sliced

1 small sweet pepper, cored, deseeded and finely diced

1 celery stalk, thinly sliced

for the marinade

2 heaped teaspoons finely chopped lemon grass

1 heaped teaspoon ground black pepper

1 tablespoon sesame oil

½ teaspoon salt

for the dressing

2 tablespoons fish sauce

1 teaspoon palm sugar

2 teaspoons lemon juice

3 small red chillies, finely chopped

3 garlic cloves, finely chopped

1 Make the marinade by mixing all the ingredients in a bowl. Add the duck and leave to marinate for 1 hour.

2 In another bowl, mix all the dressing ingredients and set aside.

3 When ready to cook, preheat a hot grill and arrange the salad on a serving platter and set aside.

4 Remove the duck from the marinade and grill the flesh side for 2 minutes to sear it, turn it over and sear the skin side for 2 minutes. Reduce the heat to moderate and cook the flesh side for another 10 minutes and the skin side for 5 minutes more. (This will produce fairly well-cooked meat, so keep an eye on timings, as you don't want to overcook it; if you prefer your duck less well cooked, then reduce the second set of timings by a few minutes on each side.) Cut the cooked duck into small cubes.

5 Place the duck in a bowl and add all the remaining salad ingredients. Stir well, add the dressing and stir well again.

6 Turn out on the salad and serve.

fried rice balls and pork skin salad nam sot kow thod

I've never seen this dish on sale in a restaurant. I'm not quite sure why, though it is quite complicated and chefs may think it's too much trouble. You can, though, usually see it at temple festivals and other celebrations, where it is considered a great treat. I recently stumbled across it at a fête held at Wat Arun, Bangkok's spectacular Temple of the Dawn beside the Chao Phraya river.

Someone must have been studying the old wall-paintings to find out how it must have been when the city was founded two centuries ago as, instead of the usual beauty contest and the inevitable disco, we were offered something unusual – traditional *Likay*, a mix of classical theatre and popular melodrama. There were kick-boxing contests, classical ballet and, of course, treats like this dish to add to the feeling of nostalgia for a time before electronic amusements and easy food.

100g (4oz) piece of pork skin
100g (4oz) minced pork
1 heaped tablespoon ginger that has been cut into thin matchsticks
4 small red shallots, thinly sliced
2 spring onions, thinly sliced into rounds
2 tablespoons fish sauce
2 teaspoons sugar
2 tablespoons lemon juice
1/2 teaspoon chilli powder
2 heaped tablespoons peanuts
coriander leaves, to garnish
lettuce leaves, to serve

for the rice balls
150g (5oz) cooked rice
1 egg
60g (2oz) minced pork
2 garlic cloves, finely chopped
1 heaped teaspoon finely chopped coriander root
1 tablespoon fish sauce
1/2 teaspoon ground black pepper
oil for deep-frying

1 First make the rice balls: place the rice in a large bowl, break in the egg and stir well. Add all the other rice ball ingredients, mix thoroughly and form into about 6 balls roughly the size of ping-pong balls. Heat the oil for deep-frying to hot but not sizzling and deep-fry the rice balls until golden brown. Drain well on kitchen paper and set aside.

2 Bring a pan of water to the boil, add the pork skin and boil for 5 minutes. Remove and cut into short thin strands. Set aside.

3 Heat 2 tablespoons water in a pan, add the minced pork and simmer until cooked through, about 2 – 3 minutes. Remove from the heat, add the pork skin strands and mix well.

4 Turn out into a bowl, add the fried rice balls and, with a fork, roughly break them up. Add all the remaining ingredients except the coriander and lettuce. Stir well, turn out on to a serving platter, garnish with coriander leaves and serve, accompanied by the lettuce leaves, which can be used to scoop up the salad.

mixed seafood salad yam chow lay

This is a classic, beloved of visitors to Thailand's famous beach resorts on Phuket and Koh Samui, but you can easily do it yourself in minutes. It is also very flexible, just use whatever seafood is available – prawns, mussels, crab, squid, clams – but try for as much variety as you can manage.

6 large lettuce leaves

275g (10oz) mixed seafood

1 onion, halved and thinly sliced

85g (3oz) Chinese celery, cut into thin matchsticks

1 young lemon grass stalk, sliced into thin rounds

2 spring onions, roughly chopped

1 heaped tablespoon thinly sliced kaffir lime leaf

for the dressing

4 garlic cloves, finely chopped

3 small red chillies, finely chopped

2 tablespoons fish sauce

1 teaspoon palm sugar

3 tablespoons lemon juice

1 Arrange the lettuce leaves on a serving plate and set aside.

2 Prepare the seafood individually: slice squid into small pieces, soak and debeard mussels (discarding any that remain open when tapped), etc. Then dip all briefly in a large pan of rapidly boiling water. When just cooked through, about 2–3 minutes, remove and discard shells from shellfish, peel and devein prawns, etc. Place in a bowl with the other salad ingredients, stir well and set aside.

3 In another bowl, mix all the dressing ingredients. Pour this over the salad, stir well, turn on to the platter and serve.

kale stem salad yam kanard

For this recipe you need Chinese kale, which you can find easily in Chinese stores (ask for *gaai laan*). For this salad we use only the stems. You could substitute broccoli stems.

100g (4oz) Chinese kale stems

85g (3oz) squid, cut into thin slices

85g (3oz) carrots, cut into thin matchsticks

85g (3oz) small peeled cooked shrimp

for the dressing

1 tablespoon fish sauce

2 tablespoons lemon juice

1 heaped teaspoon sugar

2 small red chillies, finely chopped

3 garlic cloves, finely chopped

1 tablespoon crisp-fried shallots (see page 23)

1 Peel the hard outer layer from the kale stems.

2 Bring a pan of water to the boil and blanch the kale stems for 15 seconds, drain well and place in a bowl.

3 Bring the water back to the boil and briefly blanch the squid (just put it in and then take it out), drain well and add to the bowl. Mix in the carrots and the shrimp.

4 Add all the dressing ingredients except the shallots and stir well.

5 Just before serving, stir in the fried shallots and turn out on to a plate.

laos

'On a recent visit to the capital, Vientiane, I ate at a food stall opposite the city's main temple Wat Simuang, and the meal was a memory of a cuisine that is rapidly disappearing in supposedly more sophisticated places. A large lady was busily pounding ingredients in a big earthenware mortar and, even before I smelled the pungent aroma of garlic and limes, I knew that this would be the salad that we Thais call *som tam* and the Lao know as *tam som* from *tam* to pound and *som* sour. This is the one Lao dish to have spread far beyond its home territory.'

Full-moon ceremony at the end of the long rains

boiled chicken salad
yam gai tom

1 large skinless chicken breast fillet

1 red and 1 green sweet pepper, deseeded and thinly sliced

1 onion, thinly sliced

1 cucumber, peeled, halved, deseeded and sliced into thin crescents

2 tomatoes, sliced

2 celery stalks, thinly sliced

for the dressing

3 garlic cloves

5 small red shallots

4 small green or red chillies

1 young lemon grass stalk, thinly sliced

2 tablespoons fish sauce

2 tablespoons lemon juice

2 level teaspoons sugar

1 level tablespoon finely chopped coriander leaves

1 Place the chicken breast in a pan, cover with cold water and bring to the boil. Remove from the heat, cover with a lid and leave for 10 minutes, until just cooked through.

2 Arrange the remaining salad ingredients on a serving platter.

3 Prepare the dressing: preheat a hot grill. Wrap the garlic, shallots and chillies in foil and grill the parcel for 1 minute on each side. Remove from the foil parcel, place in a mortar and pound to a paste. Mix in all the other dressing ingredients and stir well. Set aside.

4 Tear the chicken into small shreds and scatter on the serving platter. Pour over the dressing, mix well and serve.

hot and sour papaya salad
tam som

This is the classic Lao salad and a dish which, in varying forms, has now spread to neighbouring countries (in Thailand it's called *som tam*), much to the delight of vegetarian travellers, as there is nearly always a stall with some on offer at every street market and bus or train station. It is best to specify how hot you want it before pounding begins – just point to the chillies and nod or shake your head.

3 garlic cloves

4 small red or green chillies

150g (5oz) raw, green papaya, peeled and finely shredded into long strips

1 tomato, cut into wedges

1 tablespoon pickled fish (see page 24)

2 tablespoons lime juice

1 tablespoon palm sugar (see page 24)

crisp salad, to serve

1 In a mortar, pound together the garlic and chillies, then add each ingredient except the salad, pound each in turn and ensuring that it is well mixed in – the length of time depends on the texture of each, thus the papaya will need longer than the garlic.

2 When the liquids are well absorbed and the sugar dissolved, turn out on to a serving platter and serve accompanied by the salad.

salad with savoury pork sausage
yam moo som

At the noodle stall in Vientiane this was made with Lao 'sour' sausage, a mix of pork with garlic and chillies which is allowed to ferment before being cooked. There's a recipe for this in my previous book, *Vatch's Southeast Asian Cookbook*, but I've simplified things here by using Western sausage.

mixed seasonal salad
275 (10oz) small frankfurters
1 onion, thinly sliced
1 small cucumber, cut into thin matchsticks
2 tomatoes, cut into thin wedges

for the dressing
4 garlic cloves
4 small red or green chillies
2 tablespoons fish sauce
2 tablespoons lime juice
2 level teaspoons sugar

1 Arrange the salad around the edges of a serving platter and set aside.

2 Make the dressing by mixing all the ingredients in a large bowl. Set aside.

3 Heat some water in a saucepan and boil the sausages until cooked through, usually around 4 minutes. Remove from the water and slice into rounds.

4 Place the sausages in the bowl with the dressing. Add the onion, cucumber and tomato, and mix well. Turn out on to the platter and serve.

spicy minced pork salad
laap moo

150g (5oz) minced pork
1 level tablespoon galangal, finely chopped
2 tablespoons fish sauce
2 tablespoons lime juice
1 teaspoon sugar
½ teaspoon chilli powder
6 small red shallots, thinly sliced
4 spring onions, finely chopped
1 level tablespoon ground dry-fried rice (see page 23)
20 mint leaves, roughly chopped
crisp salad, to serve

1 Heat 2 tablespoons of water in a saucepan, add the minced pork and simmer until just cooked through, about 2 – 3 minutes.

2 Remove the pan from the heat, add all the other ingredients except the salad and stir well.

3 Turn out on to a plate and serve accompanied by the salad.

Lao salad salat

6 large lettuce leaves

1 cucumber, thinly sliced

1 red and 1 green sweet pepper, cored, deseeded and thinly sliced

3 hard-boiled eggs, shelled and quartered

coriander leaves, to garnish

for the dressing

175g (6oz) minced pork

2 tablespoons fish sauce

2 level teaspoons sugar

2 small red or green chillies, finely chopped

2 tablespoons lime juice

1 tablespoon garlic oil

1 heaped tablespoon ground roast peanuts

1 Arrange the lettuce, cucumber and pepper slices on a serving platter, place the egg quarters on the salad and set aside.

2 Prepare the dressing: heat 3 tablespoons of water in a pan, add the pork together with all the dressing ingredients except the garlic oil and the peanuts and simmer until the pork is just cooked through, about 2 – 3 minutes. Remove from the heat.

3 Add the garlic oil and ground peanuts, and stir well Turn out on to the salad platter, garnish with coriander leaves and serve.

bamboo shoot salad soop no mai

225g (8oz) bamboo shoots (see page 19), shredded with a fork

4 garlic cloves, finely chopped

1 tablespoon fish sauce

1 tablespoon liquid from pickled fish (see page 24)

2 tablespoons lime juice

2 level teaspoons sugar

$\frac{1}{2}$ teaspoon chilli powder

4 small shallots, thinly sliced

2 heaped tablespoons roughly chopped coriander leaves

1 level tablespoon dry-fried sesame seeds

1 level tablespoon ground dry-fried rice (see page 23)

1 Heat 2 tablespoons of water in a saucepan, add the shredded bamboo shoots and gently simmer for 1 minute.

2 Add all the remaining ingredients, stir well, turn out on to a plate and serve.

mixed salad yam noi

1 large egg

salt

1 tablespoon cooking oil

100g (4 oz) pork fillet

60g (2oz) long beans, cut into 2.5cm (1in) lengths

60g (2oz) water spinach (see page 22)

60g (2oz) beansprouts

5 large iceberg lettuce leaves

60g (2oz) cucumber, thinly sliced

60g (2oz) round aubergine, thinly sliced

10 whole peeled cooked prawns

2 heaped tablespoons roughly chopped mint leaves, to garnish

1 level tablespoon dry-fried sesame seeds (see page 23), to garnish

for the dressing

4 garlic cloves

5 small red shallots

4 small red or green chillies

2 tablespoons fish sauce

2 tablespoons lime juice

2 teaspoons sugar

1 Beat the egg with the salt. Heat the oil in a large frying pan, pour in the egg and cook to a very thin, dry omelette. Remove from the pan, roll into a cylinder and slice across thinly to make very thin strips. Set aside.

2 Place the pork in a pan, cover with water, bring to the boil and simmer until just cooked through, about 3 minutes. Remove, slice thinly and set aside.

3 Bring a pan of salted water to the boil and briefly blanch the beans, spinach and beansprouts in turn, ensuring that they each remain al dente. Arrange the lettuce, cucumber and aubergine in a serving bowl, add the pork and the prawns together with the blanched vegetables and set aside.

4 Prepare the dressing: preheat a hot grill. Wrap the garlic, shallots and chillies in foil and grill for 1 minute on each side. Remove from the foil and place in a mortar. Pound to a paste, then stir in the fish sauce, lemon juice and sugar until the sugar dissolves. Pour over the salad and mix well.

5 Mix in the omelette slices, and garnish with mint and sesame seeds.

beef salad laap sin

The original main ingredient for this is water buffalo and it's a way of using up all the bits, like intestines etc., left over when all the best cuts have been used. Despite that rather forbidding description, it is really very tasty, but utterly impractical in the West, so here's my version – without intestines!

crisp salad

275g (10oz) rump steak, grilled to taste and then thinly sliced (be sure to catch any juices)

2 heaped teaspoons galangal, finely chopped

2 tablespoons fish sauce

4 small red shallots, thinly sliced

4 small red chillies, finely chopped

3 spring onions, finely chopped

2 tablespoons lime juice

1 heaped tablespoon mint leaves, finely chopped

1 heaped tablespoon ground dry-fried rice (see page 23)

1 Arrange the salad on a serving platter and set aside.

2 Place the steak in a bowl, with any juices. Mix in the remaining ingredients, turn out on the serving platter and serve with the salad.

Opposite: Sundown at a riverside bar over the waters of the Mekong at Vientiane

minced pork and aubergine salad soop mak kheua

12 round green aubergines (eggplants)

1 tablespoon lemon juice

150g (5oz) minced pork

1 young lemon grass stalk, thinly sliced

1 heaped teaspoon grated fresh ginger

1 level tablespoon dry-fried sesame seeds, to garnish

for the dressing

4 small red shallots

3 garlic cloves

4 small red or green chillies

2 tablespoons fish sauce

1 tablespoon tamarind water (see page 25)

2 level teaspoons sugar

1 heaped tablespoon finely chopped coriander (leaf and stem)

1 Thinly slice the aubergine and place in cold water with the lemon juice.

2 Heat 2 tablespoons of water in a pan, add the minced pork, lemon grass and ginger, and simmer until the pork is cooked through, about 2 – 3 minutes, stirring well. Remove from the pan and place in a serving bowl.

3 Prepare the dressing: preheat a hot grill. Wrap the shallots, garlic and chillies in foil and grill the parcel for 1 minute on each side. Remove from the foil, place in a mortar and pound to a paste. Stir in the remaining dressing ingredients, mixing well, and pour over the pork.

4 Drain the aubergines, add to the bowl, mix well and serve, garnished with sesame seeds.

cucumber salad tam taeng

On a recent visit to Laos, a friend in the Thai Embassy in Vientiane took me for a sundowner at one of the fragile-looking wooden bars built on stilts out over the river that line the banks of the Mekong. This is one of the best things the town has to offer and such a quiet moment at the end of the working day is understandably popular. You can watch a group of friends meet up at a favourite spot and what starts as a few drinks with snacks soon develops into a full-blown meal, as more and more dishes are brought to the table.

Of course, it's the river that makes the magic. A rushing broad torrent in the rainy season; a narrow glittering trickle edging round its exposed sand banks in the dry season. The rapid descent of the sun blazing into the river is beautiful and dramatic. Little narrow boats are sculled across the shimmering, silvery surface and what look like fairy-lights start to sparkle on the opposite bank in neighbouring Thailand, so tantalizingly close.

The bar/restaurant my friend chose was the aptly named Soud Seni Luck Rim Kong, which means something like 'My Sweet Hear'', presumably because it's a pleasant spot for young lovers. Well, lovers or not, it was a good place for a cool drink and a pleasant snack. We chose spicy salads because they go so well with drinks, it's a bit like nibbling tapas in Spain. This recipe and the Spicy Fried Egg Salad are two of the dishes we tried, so open a bottle of lager and imagine its Beer Lao and you can be there by the great river.

1 large cucumber, peeled, then grated lengthwise down to the inner seeds

1 large tomato, cut into thin wedges

1 tablespoon liquid from pickled fish (see page 24)

1 tablespoon fish sauce

2 tablespoons lime juice

2 teaspoons sugar

3 small red chillies, finely chopped

1 Place all the ingredients in a bowl and mix well until the sugar dissolves. Turn out on to a plate and serve.

spicy fried egg salad yam kai dow

3 tablespoons cooking oil

4 eggs

5 lettuce leaves

1 onion, thinly sliced

1 tomato, thinly sliced

for the dressing

2 tablespoons lime juice

2 tablespoons fish sauce

2 level teaspoons sugar

4 small red or green chillies, finely chopped

5 small red shallots, thinly sliced

1 Heat the oil in a frying pan and fry the eggs, turning once to cook the yolk. Carefully remove the eggs from the pan, allow them to cool and then cut them into squares. Set aside.

2 In a bowl, prepare the dressing by mixing all the ingredients, stirring well until the sugar is dissolved. Set aside.

3 Arrange the remaining salad ingredients on a serving platter, then arrange the egg squares on top. Pour over the dressing and serve.

clear vermicelli salad yam sen ron

I really like the main market in Vientiane, Talad Kua Din, because you can still pick up true bargains and real oddities, which interest me more than antiques. Last time I was there I bought a set of old communist medals, with enamelled red stars and silhouettes of Marx and Lenin. I also found some fantastically well-crafted model motorbikes made out of nuts and bolts and other bits and pieces, apparently made in Vietnam where, during the long years of war and privation, young people mastered the art of salvaging anything and using it creatively.

There is, of course, a huge food section to the market and the surrounding neighbourhood is inevitably the best place to eat. Because of the French connection, there are plenty of stalls serving fresh baguettes with home-made Lao pâté, but I chose an unnamed noodle stall, where I had a late breakfast of sausage salad and my friend had a glass-noodle salad with pork and prawns..

60g (2oz) clear vermicelli (glass noodle)
30g (1oz) dried black fungus mushrooms
85g (3oz) minced pork
8 large raw prawns, shelled and deveined, then roughly chopped
150g (5oz) Chinese celery, cut into 5cm (2in) lengths (if you substitute
   Western celery, try to get young stems and cut them as fine as possible)
3 spring onions, thinly sliced
coriander leaves, to garnish

for the dressing
2 tablespoons fish sauce
2 tablespoons lime juice
2 level teaspoons sugar
2 garlic cloves, finely chopped
4 small red or green chillies, finely chopped

1 Soak the vermicelli noodles in cold water until soft: the very thin ones take about 10 minutes, the thicker ones nearer 15 minutes. When soft, drain and roughly chop. Set aside.

2 Soak the mushrooms in cold water until soft, about 5 minutes. Drain and roughly chop. Set aside.

3 Heat 2 tablespoons of water in a pan, add the minced pork and chopped prawns and stir well until the meat is just cooked through, about 2 – 3 minutes. Add the noodles and mushrooms, and stir well. Turn into a bowl, add the celery and spring onions and mix well.

4 Add all the dressing ingredients and stir until the sugar dissolves, turn out on to a plate, garnish with coriander leaves and serve.

mushroom salad soop hed

This is a classic 'pick-and-cook' recipe and, while I have suggested easily available oyster mushrooms, this would be wonderful with wild mushrooms – should you manage to get them safely! No one should go mushrooming without expert guidance, but there are Italian stores that occasionally stock fresh forest mushrooms.

mixed seasonal salad
275g (10oz) oyster mushrooms, preferably small but thinly sliced if large
1 onion, thinly sliced
1 tablespoon pickled fish, finely chopped (see page 24)
2 level teaspoons sugar
½ teaspoon chilli powder
2 tablespoons lime juice
3 spring onions, roughly chopped
1 heaped tablespoon finely chopped mint leaves
1 heaped tablespoon ground dry-fried rice (see page 23)

1 Arrange the salad around the outside of a serving platter and set aside.

2 Heat 2 tablespoons of water in a saucepan, add the mushrooms and simmer for a second or two. Then add all the remaining ingredients except the mint and rice, and continue to simmer for 1 minute more.

3 Remove from the heat and stir in the mint leaves and ground rice. Turn out on to the centre of the salad platter and serve.

cambodia

'When I saw the carved stone friezes on the temple walls at Angkor Wat, it wasn't the vast battles and epic scenes from ancient scriptures that gripped me most, but the little details of how people lived, especially how they cook and ate. So you can imagine my delight one lunchtime in a restaurant near the site, when I saw someone grilling a fish held in a framework of split bamboo strips, identical to one I had seen in the carvings. To experience a method of cooking food that had survived intact down the centuries was awesome, and the fact that the area around present-day Angkor is renowned for its smoked fish could mean that something similar to this recipe was eaten in the days of the Khmer empire.'

Stone carving on the walls of the Bayon, Angkor Wat, showing a method of grilling fish still used today

smoked fish with green mango salad yoam makah trey ang

When I saw the carved stone friezes on the temple walls at Angkor Wat, it wasn't the vast battles and the epic scenes from the ancient scriptures that gripped me most, but the little details of how people lived, especially how they cooked and ate. So you can imagine my delight one lunchtime in a restaurant near the site, when I saw someone grilling a fish held in a framework of split bamboo strips, identical to one I had just seen in one of the carvings. To experience a method of cooking food that had survived intact down the centuries was awesome, and the fact that the area around present-day Angkor is renowned for its smoked fish could mean that something similar to this recipe was eaten in the days of the Khmer empire.

6 large lettuce leaves
100g (4oz) smoked fish (mackerel or similar)
100g (4oz) green (unripe) mango, peeled and cut into thin matchsticks
60g (2oz) carrot, cut into thin matchsticks
3 small red shallots, finely chopped
4 small red chillies, finely chopped
2 tablespoons fish sauce
2 tablespoons lime juice
2 level teaspoons sugar
coriander leaves, to garnish

1 Arrange the lettuce leaves on a serving platter and set aside

2 Flake the smoked fish into bite-sized pieces and place in a bowl. Add all the other ingredients and stir well.

3 Turn out on to the serving platter with the lettuce leaves, garnish with coriander and serve.

spicy duck salad yoam sat tuey

You see ducks everywhere in Cambodia; they can even be a serious traffic hazard when a swarm of them suddenly waddles on to a main road heading for a nearby river, forcing you to screech to a halt. Not surprisingly, you are more likely to find duck eggs and meat on a Cambodian menu than chicken. The Rainbow Restaurant on National Road 6A, beyond Phnom Penh, is famous for its duck – ducks' feet actually! They are often served with crispy noodles at weddings, presumably because they're so plentiful. As this is not the case in other parts of the world, I've substituted the easier-to-obtain duck breast for the virtually impossible feet, though in truth I think the replacement is tastier.

crispy salad
2 duck breasts, finely chopped
1 level tablespoon galangal, finely chopped
5 small red shallots, thinly sliced
2 spring onions, thinly sliced
1 heaped tablespoon roughly chopped coriander leaves
2 tablespoons fish sauce
1 heaped teaspoon sugar
2 tablespoons lime juice
½ teaspoon chilli powder

1 Arrange the salad on a plate and set aside.

2 Heat 3 tablespoons of water in a pan, add the duck and simmer until cooked through, about 5 minutes. Remove from the heat.

3 Add all the remaining ingredients and mix well. Turn out on to a plate and serve accompanied by the salad.

chicken and banana flower salad

yoam tra yorng jay

Like the Chicken and Clear Vermicelli Salad on page 65 this is a speciality of the Special Rice Crust Restaurant on the banks of the Mekong.

1 skinless chicken breast fillet

1 young banana flower, halved

1 young lemon grass stalk, finely chopped

1 heaped tablespoon finely chopped galangal

1 tablespoon pickled fish (see page 24)

10 mint leaves, to garnish

for the dressing

5 small red shallots

3 garlic cloves

1 large dried chilli, roughly chopped

1 teaspoon shrimp paste

$\frac{1}{2}$ teaspoon salt

2 tablespoons lime juice

3 spring onions, roughly chopped

1 heaped tablespoon roughly chopped coriander leaves

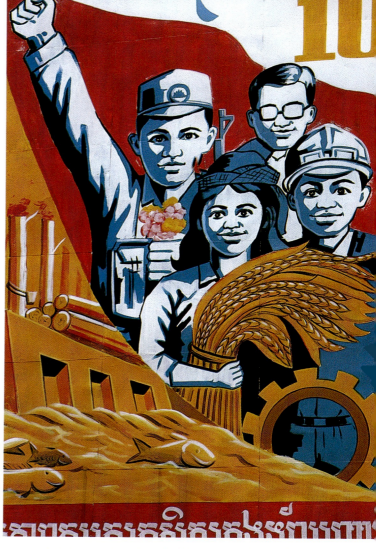

While still in communist style, a poster celebrates the tenth anniversary of the overthrow of the Khmer Rouge

1 Place the chicken breast and banana flower in a pan, just cover with water and bring to the boil. Add the lemon grass, galangal and fish pickle and simmer until the chicken is just cooked through, about 8 minutes.

2 Drain away the liquid, reserving all the boiled ingredients in a bowl. When cool enough to handle, tear the chicken and banana flower into small pieces and set aside.

3 Prepare the dressing: preheat a hot grill. Wrap the shallot, garlic, chilli and shrimp paste in foil and grill the parcel for 1 minute on each side. Turn the contents of the foil parcel into a mortar and pound to a paste. Add the salt and lime juice, and mix well.

4 Pour the dressing into the bowl with the chicken, banana flower, lemon grass and galangal, and mix well.

5 Just before serving, stir in the spring onions and coriander leaves. Turn out on to a plate, garnish with mint leaves and serve.

mushroom salad
yoam palat bang

mixed seasonal salad
1 young lemon grass stalk, thinly sliced
1 tablespoon pickled fish (see page 24)
150g (5oz) small oyster mushrooms (or similar), halved if large
3 spring onions, roughly chopped
¼ teaspoon salt
1 heaped tablespoon roughly chopped coriander
lemon slices, to serve

for the dressing
1 teaspoon shrimp paste
1 large dried chilli, roughly chopped
1 heaped teaspoon roughly chopped galangal
4 garlic cloves
1 small red shallots

1 Prepare the dressing: preheat a hot grill. Wrap all the dressing ingredients in foil and grill the parcel for 1 minute on each side. Turn the contents of the foil parcel into a mortar and pound to a paste. Set aside.

2 Arrange the salad around the edges of a serving platter and set aside.

3 Heat 3 tablespoons of water in a pan, heat, add the lemon grass and pickled fish, and bring to a simmer. Add the mushrooms and just bring back to a simmer. Add the dressing paste, stir well, remove from the heat and add the spring onions, salt and coriander. Mix well.

4 Turn out into the centre of the salad and serve with lemon slices.

crispy fish with green tomato salad
yoam pengpok dri cha'aa

On its home territory this dish would probably be made with catfish, which is thin and very easy to crisp. Cambodian friends told me this was such a basic part of their cuisine, virtually on every menu across the land, they insisted I include it. I've suggested a river fish to keep as close to the original as possible.

6 large lettuce leaves
3 green tomatoes, sliced into small wedges
oil for deep-frying
1 medium trout or similar firm fish, cleaned and filleted

for the dressing
2 tablespoons fish sauce
2 tablespoons lime juice
1 level tablespoon palm sugar
4 garlic cloves, finely chopped
3 small shallots, finely chopped
4 small red or green chillies, finely chopped

1 Arrange the lettuce and tomato on a serving platter and set aside.

2 Heat the oil for deep-frying to hot but not sizzling and fry the whole trout fillets until crispy. Drain on kitchen paper, place on the salad and set aside.

3 Mix all the dressing ingredients in a bowl until the sugar dissolves. Pour over the fish and serve.

fried beef with green papaya salad
cha sat chalu lahung

In Cambodia this would probably be based on buffalo, which is thought to have 'sweeter' meat.

275g (10oz) entrecôte steak, sliced across the grain into 2.5cm (1in) strips
oil for deep-frying
150g (5oz) green (raw) papaya, finely shredded
85g (3oz) long beans, cut into 2.5cm (1in) lengths
1 heaped tablespoon ground roast peanuts
1 heaped tablespoon ground dried shrimp (see page 23)

for the marinade
3 tablespoons fish sauce
1 tablespoon sesame oil
2 level teaspoons sugar
$\frac{1}{2}$ teaspoon ground black pepper

for the dressing
3 garlic cloves, finely chopped
3 small red chillies, finely chopped
2 tablespoons fish sauce
2 level teaspoons sugar
2 tablespoons lime juice

1 Mix all the marinade ingredients in a shallow dish, add the strips of steak, toss to coat well and leave to marinate for 3 hours.

2 Remove the meat from the marinade. Heat the oil to sizzling-hot and briefly deep-fry the steak strips until lightly browned. Turn out on to a plate and set aside.

3 Place the papaya and long beans in a bowl, add all the dressing ingredients and stir well.

4 Just before serving, add the ground peanuts and dried shrimp. Stir, turn out on to a plate and serve accompanied by the plate of fried beef.

prawn with long bean salad
sadak gua bok

mixed seasonal salad
175g (6oz) long beans, cut into 5cm (2in) lengths
8 raw king prawns, shelled and deveined
2 tablespoons coconut cream
1 heaped tablespoon ground roast peanuts

for the dressing
4 small red shallots
3 garlic cloves
2 large dried chillies, roughly chopped
2 tablespoon fish sauce
2 teaspoons tamarind water (see page 25)
1 teaspoon palm sugar

1 First prepare the dressing: preheat a hot grill. Wrap the shallot, garlic and chillies in foil and grill the parcel for 1 minute on each side. Turn the contents of the foil parcel into a mortar and pound to a paste. Add the remaining dressing ingredients and stir well until the sugar dissolves. Set aside.

2 Arrange the salad on a serving platter and set aside.

3 Bring a pan of water to the boil and briefly blanch the long beans, drain and turn into a bowl.

4 Bring the water back to the boil and briefly dip in the prawns until they just change colour. Drain and turn into the bowl.

5 Add the dressing and stir well. Turn out on to the platter with the salad, pour over the coconut cream and the ground peanuts and serve.

white cabbage with prawn salad
yoam sapai braadok gia muay bongkia

175g (6oz) white cabbage, finely shredded
8 peeled cooked prawns
2 tablespoons coconut milk
1 heaped tablespoon crisp-fried shallots (see page 23)

for the dressing
4 small red shallots
3 large garlic cloves
2 large dried chillies, roughly chopped
2 tablespoons fish sauce
2 level teaspoons sugar
2 tablespoons lime juice

1 Place the cabbage and prawns in a bowl and set aside.

2 Prepare the dressing: preheat a hot grill. Wrap the shallots, garlic and chillies in foil and grill the parcel for 1 minute on each side. Turn the contents of the foil parcel into a mortar and pound to a paste. Stir in the remaining dressing ingredients, mix well and pour over the salad. Mix well again.

3 Just before serving, stir in the coconut milk and fried shallots, turn out on to a plate and serve.

1 Place the salad in a bowl and set aside.

2 Preheat a moderate grill and grill the sweet peppers, chillies, shallots and garlic until the skins of the sweet peppers are blackened and blistered. Remove from the heat and peel away the loose skins. Cut all the grilled vegetables into thin slices, place in the bowl with the salad and set aside.

3 In another bowl, mix all the dressing ingredients, pour over the salad and mix well.

4 Just before serving, stir in the dried shrimp and turn out on to a plate. Place the egg on top of the salad, garnish with coriander leaves and serve.

egg and sweet pepper salad
yoam pong sungao mat tet

Sweet peppers are quite rare and expensive in Cambodia, so this dish is something of a luxury there. I've simply suggested ordinary red or green peppers, but you could mix a whole range of varieties and colours to make a highly decorative dish.

mixed seasonal salad

3 medium red or green sweet peppers

2 large red chillies

4 small red shallots

4 large garlic cloves

1 heaped tablespoon ground dried shrimp (see page 23), to garnish

2 hard-boiled eggs, shelled and quartered

coriander leaves, to garnish

for the dressing

2 tablespoons fish sauce

1 teaspoon palm sugar

2 tablespoons lime juice

cucumber salad yoam droksok

1 large cucumber, halved lengthwise, deseeded and cut across into 1cm (¹⁄₂in) pieces

6 small red onions, thinly sliced

1 heaped tablespoon finely chopped mint leaves

1 heaped tablespoon ground roast peanuts

1 heaped tablespoon crisp-fried garlic (see page 23)

for the dressing

2 tablespoons white vinegar

2 level teaspoons sugar

1 tablespoon fish sauce

3 small red chillies, finely chopped

1 Place the salad ingredients in a bowl, add the dressing ingredients and stir.

2 Just before serving, stir in the peanuts and garlic, and turn out on to a plate.

chicken and clear vermicelli salad
nheam moan

I ate this in Phnom Penh, in the wonderfully named Special Rice Crust Restaurant, one of a line of relatively new large eating houses that line the Mekong, just beyond the city across the Cambodian/Japanese Friendship Bridge, along Porimphorn Road. It seems that everyone who can likes to drive out there in the evening, turning this into one of the capital's main food areas. There always seem to be boisterous parties – weddings or groups of office workers on a spree – and many of these vast hangar-like places have live music and other entertainment. Personally, I prefer a quiet corner where I can eat in peace and watch the passing traffic on the river.

85g (3oz) white cabbage, finely shredded
1 carrot, sliced into thin matchsticks
85g (3oz) beansprouts
60g (2oz) (dry weight) clear vermicelli (glass noodles)
1 tablespoon oil
1 heaped tablespoon dried shrimp
1 skinless chicken breast fillet, very finely chopped (as if minced)
2 level tablespoons ground roast peanuts

for the dressing
2 garlic cloves, finely chopped
3 small red chillies, finely chopped
2 tablespoons fish sauce
2 level teaspoons sugar
2 tablespoons lime juice

1 Place the cabbage, carrot and beansprouts in a bowl and set aside. Soak the clear vermicelli in water until soft, about 15 minutes, then drain them and roughly chop. Set aside.

2 Heat the oil in a small frying pan and fry the dried shrimp until crispy. Drain on kitchen paper and set aside.

3 Heat 3 tablespoons of water in a pan, add the chicken and simmer until cooked, about 3 minutes. Stir in the vermicelli and remove from the heat.

4 Add all dressing ingredients and stir well. Pour over the salad and mix well.

5 Just before serving, stir in the crisp-fried shrimps and the peanuts.

hot and sour beef salad
plea saj go

mixed seasonal salad
225g (8oz) rump steak
1 young lemon grass stalk, thinly sliced
1 onion, halved and thinly sliced
85g (3oz) cucumber, halved lengthwise and then thinly sliced across
2 small red chillies, finely chopped
2 tablespoons fish sauce
2 level teaspoons sugar
2 tablespoons lime juice
about 10 mint leaves, to garnish

1 Arrange the salad on a serving platter and set aside. Preheat a medium-to-hot grill and grill the steak to taste (3 – 5 minutes on each side for medium-rare), reserving any juices.

2 Cut the steak into thin slices and place in a bowl with the juices. Mix in all the remaining ingredients. Turn out on to the platter with the salad and garnish.

mussel salad

yoam grum kachong

I didn't see mussels in Phnom Penh, but they do have shellfish brought up from the coast; in particular, the mud-clams that are gathered at low tide all round the Southeast Asian coastline. You could, however, use any shellfish here and mussels are probably easiest to find. I ate a clam version of this recipe at Rum Chon, another out-of-town restaurant, a bit further on from the main group, about 4 kilometres after the Japanese bridge.

mixed seasonal salad

450g (1lb) mussels, soaked, cleaned and debearded

1 heaped tablespoon ginger, cut into thin matchsticks

5 small red shallots, thinly sliced

3 small red chillies, finely chopped

2 teaspoon tamarind water (see page 25)

1 tablespoon fish sauce

1 heaped teaspoon sugar

3 spring onions, roughly chopped

5 kaffir lime leaves, rolled together and then thinly sliced into slivers

1 Arrange the salad on a serving platter and set aside.

2 Cover the bottom of a large pan with 2.5cm (1in) water. Bring to the boil. Discard any mussels that have opened in the cleaning water and which do not close again when tapped; place the remainder in the pan. Cover and bring to the boil, agitating the pan to keep the mussels moving. Continue cooking for a minute or two, until all the mussels have opened. Discard any which have not.

3 Remove the mussels from their shells, place in a bowl and add all the remaining ingredients. Mix well and turn out on to the platter with the salad to serve.

salad with duck egg omelette

yoam pong jian

Being Cambodian, this dish calls for ducks' eggs, but if these are hard to find you could use hens' eggs.

1 medium cucumber, halved lengthwise, deseeded and sliced into thin matchsticks
4 spring onions, cut into 2.5cm (1in) lengths
2 tomatoes, cut into wedges
3 large duck eggs
2 teaspoons lime juice
1 tablespoon cooking oil
coriander leaves, to garnish

for the dressing
2 tablespoons fish sauce
1 heaped teaspoon sugar
2 tablespoons lime juice
3 garlic cloves, finely chopped
3 small red chillies, finely chopped

1 In a bowl, mix all the dressing ingredients and set aside.

2 Place the cucumber, spring onions and tomatoes in another bowl.

3 Break the eggs into a third bowl, add the lime juice and beat thoroughly.

4 Heat the oil in a frying pan, add the eggs and cook a thick, solid Spanish-style omelette. Turn out, allow to cool and then cut into 2.5cm (1in) cubes.

5 Place the omelette cubes in the bowl with the salad. Pour over the dressing and mix well. Turn out on to a plate, garnish with coriander and serve.

vietnam

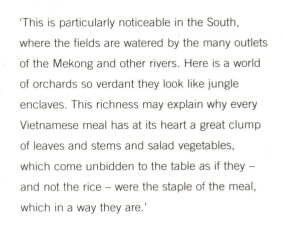

'This is particularly noticeable in the South, where the fields are watered by the many outlets of the Mekong and other rivers. Here is a world of orchards so verdant they look like jungle enclaves. This richness may explain why every Vietnamese meal has at its heart a great clump of leaves and stems and salad vegetables, which come unbidden to the table as if they – and not the rice – were the staple of the meal, which in a way they are.'

Deftly handled longboats in the Mekong delta

grilled beef salad   goi bo

Pavement dining is a big thing in Saigon, though everything associated with it is tiny: tiny little stools – on which diners squat only a little above ground level, clustered around a small portable gas ring on which dishes like this are prepared. You can sometimes find alleyways completely blocked by these supposedly temporary eating places, which clearly become permanent features in some neighbourhoods. They can be very lively, with crowds of city workers enjoying lunch or an end-of-the-day get-together. The only big thing is the amount of salad everyone eats, with huge plastic tubs stacked with leaves and plants waiting to replenish the fast-emptying plates.

450g (1lb) fillet steak, about 2.5 (1in) thick
175g (6oz) beansprouts
20 holy basil leaves
20 mint leaves
green salad in season, equivalent to 6 large lettuce leaves

for the marinade
5 tablespoons lime juice
4 tablespoons fish sauce
2 tablespoons sugar
2 young lemon grass stalks, sliced paper-thin
2 small chillies, finely chopped

1 First make the marinade: in a bowl, whisk together the lime juice, fish sauce and sugar until the sugar is completely dissolved. Add the lemon grass and chillies, and let stand for 20 minutes.

2 Preheat a moderate-to-hot grill and grill the steak for 1 to 2 minutes each side, depending on personal preference. Transfer to a cutting surface and slice thinly.

3 Add the sliced steak to the marinade, turn to coat well and leave for 30 minutes.

4 Arrange the beansprouts, herbs and salad in a bowl or deep platter. Pile the marinated beef at the centre and pour over all the marinade juices. Either toss the salad now or bring it to the table and toss there, and serve.

chicken salad ga xe phay

spicy squid salad goi mue

To judge by the frequency with which I encountered this salad on my journeys around the country, I can only assume that is one of Vietnam's most popular dishes. Those wary of chilli and other hot spices can feel safe with this, as the taste is more sweet-and-sour than hot.

450g (1lb) skinless chicken breast fillet
225g (8oz) cabbage, roughly chopped into matchsticks
1 large carrot, chopped into fine matchsticks
½ teaspoon salt
1 large shallot, thinly sliced
1 large garlic clove, finely chopped
2 small chillies, finely chopped
20 mint leaves, roughly chopped
2 tablespoons chopped roasted peanuts, to garnish

for the dressing
2 tablespoons fish sauce
2 tablespoons lime juice
1 tablespoon rice (or white) vinegar
2 teaspoons sugar

1 Place the chicken in a pan, cover with cold water and bring to the boil. Remove from the heat, cover and leave for 10 minutes until just cooked through. With your fingers, shred the meat into small pieces and set aside.

2 Make the dressing by whisking all the ingredients together in a large bowl. Add the cabbage, carrots and salt and set aside.

3 Arrange the shallots, garlic, chillies and mint leaves in a bowl, then add the vegetables and dressing, followed by the shredded chicken. Toss well.

4 Garnish with chopped peanuts to serve.

1 medium-sized (450g/1lb) squid, skinned and cleaned
1 large tomato, sliced into thin wedges
20 holy basil leaves
1 large onion, sliced into thin wedges
1 tablespoon dry-fried white sesame seeds (see page 23)
coriander leaves, to garnish

for the dressing
2 tablespoons fish sauce
4 tablespoons lime juice
1 tablespoon sugar
1 large garlic clove, finely chopped
2 or more small chillies, finely chopped

1 Preheat a hot grill. Spread the squid on a cutting board and, with a sharp knife, cut a light criss-cross pattern over it. Grill each side for 3 – 4 minutes, then cut the squid into narrow strips about 2.5 cm (1in) wide. These will curl up into attractively patterned morsels. Set aside.

2 Place all the remaining salad ingredients in a bowl and add the reserved squid.

3 Make the dressing by whisking all the ingredients together in a bowl and pour over the salad.

4 Toss well, garnish with coriander and serve.

prawn and green mango salad
goi xoai xanh tom hap

I was offered this, the Pomelo Salad opposite and the Tropical Fruit Salad on page 85 during a boat tour of the Mekong delta, south of Saigon. A feature of the tour is a visit to some of the incredibly lush orchards on the tiny islands that cluster round the eight mouths of the mighty river. All manner of tropical fruits flourish along well-irrigated channels and it is an obvious move to mix these fruits with the abundant seafood available in the adjacent tidal waters.

12 raw prawns
100g (4oz) raw green mango, chopped into fine matchsticks
60g (2oz) carrots, chopped into fine matchsticks

for the garnish
2 tablespoons cooking oil
1 medium shallot, thinly sliced

for the dressing
1 tablespoon sugar
2 tablespoons hot water
1 tablespoon lime juice
2 tablespoons fish sauce
2 garlic cloves, finely chopped
2 red chillies, finely chopped

1 First prepare the garnish: heat the oil in a wok or frying pan and fry the shallot until golden brown. Drain well on kitchen paper and set aside.

2 Heat a little water in a pan. When it is boiling, add the prawns and remove as soon as they turn pink. Refresh in cold water, drain and set aside.

3 Make the dressing: dissolve the sugar in the hot water and then add all the remaining dressing ingredients, whisk together and set aside.

4 Shell and devein the reserved prawns and place them in a bowl with the mango and carrots. Pour over the dressing and toss well.

5 Turn out on to a serving dish and garnish with the fried shallot to serve.

egg salad rau tron don gian

1 small lettuce, finely shredded
100g (4oz) cucumber, peeled and cut lengthwise into strips about 7.5-
    10cm (3-4in) long
100g (4oz) carrot, peeled and lengthwise into strips 7.5-10cm (3-4in)
100g (4oz) beansprouts
2 tablespoons chopped mint leaves
2 tablespoons dry-fried sunflower seeds (see page 23)
2 hard-boiled eggs, shelled and thinly sliced

for the dressing
2 tablespoons fish sauce
2 tablespoons lemon juice
1 tablespoon white wine vinegar
2 garlic cloves, finely chopped
1 teaspoon sugar
2 small red chillies, finely chopped

1 First make the dressing: mix all the ingredients in a small bowl.

2 Arrange the lettuce, vegetables and mint in a serving bowl, add the dry-fried sunflower seeds and the dressing, and toss well.

3 Arrange the egg slices on top of the tossed salad and serve.

60g (2oz) skinless chicken breast fillet

2 tablespoons cooking oil

1 medium shallot, thinly sliced

1 medium pomelo

60g (2oz) carrot, chopped into fine matchsticks

60g (2oz) cucumber, chopped into fine matchsticks

20 mint leaves, finely chopped

2 tablespoons ground peanuts

1 tablespoon finely chopped coriander leaves

2 small red chillies, finely chopped

60g (2oz) prepared white crab meat

for the dressing

2 tablespoons hot water

1 tablespoon sugar

1 tablespoon rice vinegar

2 tablespoons fish sauce

1 Steam the chicken breast until cooked through, about 8 minutes. Leave to cool, then, using the fingers, shred into small pieces and set aside.

2 While the chicken is cooking, heat the cooking oil in a wok or frying pan and fry the sliced shallot until golden brown. Drain well and set aside.

3 Start preparing the dressing: in a saucepan, heat the water and dissolve the sugar in it. Set aside.

4 Peel the pomelo and remove any rind. Break apart the segments, then break them again into smaller pieces – you will need 150g (5oz). Place the pomelo pieces in a bowl with the carrot, cucumber, mint, peanuts, coriander, chillies, crab, fried shallot and the reserved chicken.

5 Finish the dressing: add the rice vinegar and fish sauce to the dissolved sugar liquid and stir well. Pour the dressing over the salad, toss well and serve.

pomelo salad goi buoi

I was offered this in the fascinating surroundings of a Chinese mansion in the French "colonial" style that had been built in the pre-communist era by a rich landlord. A Chinese-Vietnamese family still clung on, surrounded by the remnants of their heavy carved-wood Chinese furniture, including an ancestor shrine and other precious family heirlooms. My host watched as I sampled this refreshing dish, pointing out the bullet holes in the ceiling, a souvenir of an American air raid during the Tet offensive. On a heat-hazy tropical afternoon, such a thing seemed impossible to imagine.

vegetarian spring rolls with rice vermicelli salad bun cha gio

I ate this on my first day in Ho Chi Minh City, in an up-to-the-minute fast-food restaurant near the central market, called Pho 2000, as shiny and brightly coloured as a McDonald's yet still serving the traditional *pho* noodles with salad. There were hundreds of cyclos (bicycle rickshaws) parked outside, which always makes me wonder how there can ever be enough customers for them. Still, they must earn something because you always see them near noodle stalls, their drivers sampling the cooking while they wait to be hired. It's pretty scary, hurtling through the rush-hour traffic, head on with your chauffeur behind you, but you have to try it at least once.

100g (4oz) (soaked weight) rice vermicelli
100g (4oz) lettuce leaves, roughly chopped
85g (3oz) beansprouts
85g (3oz) cucumber, chopped into fine matchsticks
2 tablespoons ground peanuts
1 tablespoon roughly chopped coriander leaves

for the spring rolls
60g (2oz) black fungus mushrooms, finely chopped
85g (3oz) (soaked weight) rice vermicelli, finely chopped
1 garlic clove, finely chopped
1 tablespoon finely chopped coriander leaves
1 tablespoon finely chopped peanuts
1/4 teaspoon salt
1/4 teaspoon pepper
10 mint leaves, finely chopped
10 small spring roll sheets
a little flour-and-water paste
oil for deep-frying

for the dressing
4 tablespoons rice vinegar
2 tablespoons sugar
30g (1oz) carrot, sliced into thin matchsticks
30g (1oz) white radish (mooli), sliced into thin matchsticks
1/4 teaspoon salt
1 tablespoon fish sauce
2 small chillies, finely chopped

1 First prepare the spring rolls by mixing all the ingredients except the spring roll sheets, flour-and-water paste and oil in a bowl, using your hands to form a thick paste. Spread a spring roll sheet on the work surface. Place a heaped teaspoon of the mixture at the centre of the sheet and fold in three of the corners to make an open envelope. Roll the envelope towards the unopened corner and seal down the flap with a dab of the flour-and-water paste. Set aside. Repeat the procedure until you have 10 spring rolls.

2 Bring a large pan of water to the boil and dip the rice vermicelli noodles in it for 1 minute only. Drain and cool under cold running water. Drain again and arrange with the other salad ingredients in a large bowl. Set aside.

3 Make the dressing: heat the rice vinegar in a small pan and dissolve the sugar in it. Leave to cool. In a bowl, mix the carrot, white radish and salt. Set aside. When the vinegar and sugar have cooled, add the mixed salted vegetables, stir well and leave for 30 minutes. Next add the fish sauce and chillies, stir well and set aside.

4 Heat the oil for deep-frying to very hot and fry the spring rolls in batches of 3 or 4 at a time until golden brown. Drain and set aside.

5 Pour the dressing over the salad and toss well. Arrange the deep-fried spring rolls on the tossed salad and serve.

'... as shiny and brightly coloured as a McDonald's yet still serving the traditional *pho* noodles with salad'

grilled pork with rice noodle salad bun thit nuong

For this dish, everyone squats on low stools around a charcoal burner that is used to barbecue the meat. It's great fun cooking and eating together and, of course, everything is incredibly fresh.

450g (1lb) pork loin, sliced across the grain into very thin strips

275g (10oz) (soaked weight) rice noodles

100g (4oz) beansprouts

100g (4oz) carrots, chopped into fine matchsticks

100g (4oz) white radish (mooli), chopped into fine matchsticks

100g (4oz) cucumber, chopped into fine matchsticks

30 basil leaves

1 star fruit, thinly sliced across to make star-shaped leaves

for the marinade

1 large garlic clove, finely chopped

1 young lemon grass stalk, finely chopped

1 teaspoon five-spice powder

2 tablespoons fish sauce

1 teaspoon sugar

1 teaspoon sesame oil

for the dressing

1 teaspoon sugar

6 tablespoons hot water

2 tablespoons fermented anchovy sauce (see page 24)

2 tablespoons vinegar

1 garlic clove, finely chopped

2 small red chillies finally chopped

1 In a bowl, mix together the marinade ingredients, stirring well. Add the pork strips, toss to coat well and leave to marinate for 30 minutes.

2 Bring a large pan of water to the boil. Dip the rice noodles in it for 1 minute. Remove and hold under cold running water to stop the cooking process. Drain again and leave to cool.

3 Make the dressing: dissolve the sugar in the hot water, add all the other dressing ingredients, stir well and set aside.

4 Arrange the rice noodles and the remaining salad ingredients in a bowl or deep serving platter and set aside.

5 Preheat a very hot barbecue, grill or griddle pan. Cook the pork slices for 3 seconds only on each side and place on a warmed serving dish.

6 At the same time, pour the dressing over the salad, toss well and serve along with the pork.

banana blossom salad with duck and ginger dressing
goi vit bap chuoi

iced water

1 banana flower (see page 19)

1 tablespoon lemon juice

2 duck breasts

for the dressing

2 teaspoons sugar

5 tablespoons hot water

2 tablespoons rice vinegar

2 tablespoons fish sauce

1 tablespoon lime juice

2 garlic cloves, finely chopped

1 large red chilli, finely chopped

1 tablespoon finely chopped ginger

for the garnish

1 tablespoon ground roast peanut

1 tablespoon crisp-fried shallot (see page 23)

1 Have ready a large bowl of iced water. Pull away the hard outer petals from the banana flower and discard, together with any embryonic bananas, which will look like clusters of large matchsticks. Inside is a pale soft bulb, which should be quartered then sliced across into thin strips. Immediately place these in the iced water with the lemon juice. Leave for 30 minutes to draw out any sticky liquid from the leaves.

2 Place the duck breasts in a pan of cold water, bring to the boil and simmer until cooked through, about 5 – 7 minutes. Turn off the heat and pour away the water, but leave the duck breasts in the pan, covered, for 10 minutes to allow them to tenderize. When cool, remove the skin and, using your fingers, tear the meat into shreds. Set aside.

3 Prepare the dressing: in a bowl, dissolve the sugar in the hot water. Add all the other dressing ingredients and mix well. Set aside.

4 Drain the banana flower strips well and arrange in a serving bowl. Add the duck followed by the dressing and toss well Garnish with ground roast peanut and fried shallot to serve.

Young Vietnamese, wearing the traditional *ao dai* split dress, at a rehearsal for the unveiling of another statue to 'Uncle' Ho Chi Minh

fried fish with lemon grass and salad ca chien xa

I was told I must eat at Lemongrass, one of the most famous restaurants in Saigon, but the night that I went there it looked depressingly empty, and when I continued down Dong Khoi street I stumbled on the Vietnam House, which was bustling with locals and tourists and was in every way a fortunate discovery. The two-storey restaurant occupies an old French townhouse and the old-world charm is reinforced by the waiters and waitresses who wear elegant Vietnamese town costumes – the women in the *svelte* side-split *ao dai*, which, as they say, covers everything and reveals everything. Many of the dishes, like the stewed pork in a clay pot, were Vietnamese adaptations of Chinese *haute cuisine*, but this recipe, a house speciality, was pure Saigon.

1 whole trout, about 450g (1lb), cleaned and filleted
1 egg
1 young lemon grass stalk, finely chopped
½ teaspoon salt
½ teaspoon pepper
1 tablespoon light soy sauce
oil for deep-frying
5 heaped tablespoons breadcrumbs
about 10 large mixed lettuce leaves, Cos, frisée, radicchio, etc.

for the fresh pickle
6 tablespoons rice vinegar
2 tablespoons sugar
100g (4oz) carrot, cut into small cubes
100g (4oz) cucumber, cut into small cubes
1 large red chilli, thinly sliced into rounds

1 First make the fresh pickle: warm the vinegar in a small pan and dissolve the sugar in it. Pour into a small bowl and, when cool, add the carrot, cucumber and chilli. Stir well and set aside.

2 Cut the fish fillets across into thin strips roughly 7.5x2cm (3x3¾in) at the widest point. Set aside.

3 Beat the egg in a mixing bowl, add the lemon grass, salt, pepper and light soy sauce and whisk together.

4 Heat the oil for deep-frying to moderate-to-hot. Dip the fish slices in the egg mixture, roll in the breadcrumbs and then deep-fry until golden brown. Drain on kitchen paper.

5 Arrange the mixed leaves in a bowl, add the reserved fish slices and fresh pickle, toss and serve.

minced pork, prawn and pineapple

salad thit con tom xay tron dua an voi nuoc xot ca

225g (8oz) lean minced pork

225g (8oz) cooked prawns, finely chopped

2 tablespoons fish sauce

2 tablespoons lemon juice

1 teaspoon sugar

½ teaspoon chilli powder

2 tablespoons finely chopped spring onion

4 tablespoons pineapple that has been diced into small cubes about 1cm (½in) square

1 tablespoon finely slivered ginger

2 tablespoons finely chopped coriander

2 tablespoons ground roasted peanuts

10 firm lettuce leaves, to serve

1 Bring 2 tablespoons of water to the boil in a saucepan, add the pork and boil until it is cooked through, about 5 minutes. Add all the other ingredients, lower the heat and simmer for 5 minutes more.

2 Put a dollop of the mixture on each lettuce leaf and serve as canapés.

jellyfish, chicken and cucumber salad

dua leo tron voi su vathit ga

For those who can face it, dried jellyfish may be bought in Oriental stores.

100g (4oz) dried jellyfish

1 skinless chicken breast fillet

150g (5oz) cucumber, peeled and sliced lengthwise into thin strips

1 tablespoon roughly chopped fresh mint

1 tablespoon roughly chopped coriander leaves

2 tablespoons ground roasted peanuts

1 tablespoon dry-fried sesame seeds (see page 23)

for the dressing

2 teaspoons sugar

3 tablespoons hot water

2 tablespoons fish sauce

2 tablespoons light soy sauce

2 tablespoons lime juice

2 garlic cloves, finely chopped

2 dried red chillies, finely chopped

1 Put the dried jellyfish in a bowl of hot water and leave for 30 minutes. Then pour away the water, replace with fresh cold water and soak for 1 hour to remove the salt. Drain and cut into small strips about 5cm (2in) long.

2 Place the chicken in a pan of cold water, bring to the boil and simmer for 5 minutes. Turn off the heat, pour away the water and leave the chicken covered for 10 minutes to let it tenderize. Tear it into small pieces and set aside.

3 Make the dressing: dissolve the sugar in the hot water and stir in the other ingredients. Arrange the herbs, peanuts and sesame seeds in a bowl, add the jellyfish, chicken and dressing. Toss well and serve.

crab salad with crispy noodles

goi gia

oil for deep-frying

60g (2oz) (soaked weight) rice noodles

150g (5oz) prepared crab meat

100g (4oz) beansprouts

1 small iceberg lettuce, roughly chopped into strips

3 large spring onions, roughly chopped

1 large tomato, thinly sliced

20 mint leaves, roughly chopped

for the dressing

3 tablespoons sesame oil

2 small red chillies, finely chopped

1 tablespoon ginger that has been chopped into extra-thin matchsticks

2 tablespoons fish sauce

1 tablespoon lime juice

1 Heat the oil for deep-frying to hot but not sizzling and deep-fry the well-drained noodles until crispy and golden-brown. Drain on kitchen paper.

2 Mix the crab meat and beansprouts together in a bowl. Set aside.

3 Make the dressing: mix together all the ingredients in a small bowl.

4 Arrange the lettuce, spring onions, tomato and mint in a serving bowl. Add the crispy noodles and the crab meat and beansprout mixture.

5 Just before serving, add the dressing, mix well and serve at once before the crispy noodles soften.

tropical fruit salad
hua qua tron

It seems appropriate to finish the Vietnamese recipes with another dish offered to me during my boat tour of the Mekong delta, which was definitely one of the best experiences I've had in the country. The delta is beautiful and the old colonial mansions have a charm that evokes another age.

1 small pineapple, peeled, cored and cubed

1 ripe mango, peeled, sliced from stone and roughly chopped

2 large bananas, cut into thin rounds

10 lychees, outer shells and stones removed, then quartered

1 orange, peeled, broken into segments and roughly chopped

for the dressing

600ml (1 pint) water

6 tablespoons sugar

2 tablespoons finely chopped ginger

2 pieces of star anise

1 cinnamon stick

1 clove

1 tablespoon lemon juice

10 mint leaves, finely chopped

1 First make the dressing: heat the water and dissolve the sugar, then add all the other ingredients except the lemon juice and mint. Stir well and leave to cool.

2 Arrange the fruit in a serving bowl. Add the lemon juice and chopped mint to the dressing. Stir well, add to the salad and mix well.

3 Chill in the fridge before serving.

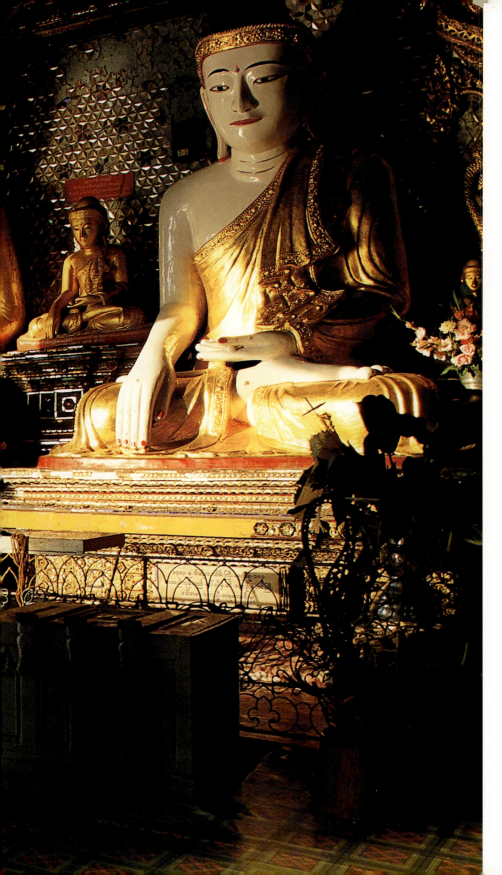

burma

'As regards salads I like the Burmese approach – one word for salad is *a thoke*, which simply means 'mix', while a word for more complex dishes, usually eaten on their own, *letthoke*, means 'mixed by hand', which is both picturesque and all-inclusive. At one end of the spectrum, plain uncooked plants served with rice and flavoured with nothing more than a dribble of fish sauce or a touch of chilli paste; at the other, a mix of blanched vegetables with cooked meat or fish, and a range of spices. The unifying elements are freshness and firmness, cooked on occasions but always swiftly and lightly...'

A monk meditating in the Two-pice Pavilion, the Shwedagon Pagoda, Rangoon

mushroom and prawn salad

pazun gyawthoke

for the salad

30g (1oz) dried fungus mushrooms, soaked in warm water (see page 22)
  then sliced into thin strips

10 peeled cooked prawns (leaving their tails on, if you prefer)

1 onion, thinly sliced

1 small cucumber, deseeded and sliced into thin matchsticks

60g (2oz) celery, sliced into thin matchsticks

1 small carrot, sliced into thin matchsticks

2 spring onions, thinly sliced into rounds

2 level teaspoons dry-fried sesame seeds (see page 23)

for the dressing

4 small red shallots

4 garlic cloves

3 small red chillies

2 tablespoons fish sauce

2 tablespoons lemon juice

2 teaspoons sugar

1 Bring a pan of water to the boil and blanch the mushroom strips in it for a few seconds. Drain well and place in a serving bowl. Add the remaining salad ingredients and set aside.

2 Prepare the dressing: preheat a hot grill. Wrap the shallots, garlic and chillies in foil and grill the parcel for 1 minute on each side. Remove from the foil, place in a mortar and pound to a paste. Add the fish sauce, lemon juice and sugar. Mix well then pour over the salad.

3 Mix the salad and dressing well and serve.

Painted statue of a praying devotee in the Shwezigan Pagoda, Pagan

green papaya salad
thinnbaw-thee thoke

150g (5oz) green papaya, peeled and grated into long thin strips

for the dressing
2 tablespoons groundnut oil
3 garlic cloves, thinly sliced
1 heaped tablespoon small dried shrimp
4 small dried chillies, roughly chopped
2 tablespoons fish sauce
2 teaspoons tamarind water (see page 25)
2 teaspoons sugar
1 heaped tablespoon ground roast peanuts

1 Arrange the papaya shreds in a salad bowl and set aside.

2 Prepare the dressing: heat the oil in a wok or frying pan and fry the garlic until golden-brown. Remove and place in the salad bowl. Then fry the dried shrimp in the same way, remove and place in the salad bowl. Finally fry the chillies, remove and place in the salad bowl with all the remaining oil in the pan.

3 Add the fish sauce, tamarind water, sugar and ground peanuts to the salad bowl. Mix well and serve.

ginger salad gin thoke

A classic Burmese salad made with fermented tea leaves is often given as a goodwill gesture after an argument or to welcome new arrivals to refresh them after their journey. Sadly, the ingredients are rarely available in the West, but the Burmese have this alternative and, like the tea leaf salad, it is also used like Western sorbet, to refresh the taste buds during a highly flavoured meal.

Leg rowers taking part in the Phaung Paw U Festival on Lake Inle

150g (5oz) young fresh ginger, peeled and sliced into thin matchsticks
2 tablespoons lime juice
½ teaspoon salt
1 tablespoon cooking oil
3 garlic cloves, thinly sliced
2 small fresh chillies, finely chopped
2 tablespoons ground dried shrimp
2 tablespoons ground roast peanuts
1 tablespoon dry-fried sesame seeds (see page 23)
1 tablespoon fish sauce
1 tablespoon lime juice
6 lettuce leaves, to serve

1 The day before, put the ginger, lime juice and salt in a bowl. Mix well, cover and leave for 24 hours.

2 Lift out the ginger with your hand and squeeze out as much of the liquid as possible. Set aside.

3 Heat the oil in a wok or frying pan and fry the garlic until crisp and golden-brown. Set aside.

4 In a bowl, mix the ginger, oil and garlic. Add each remaining ingredient in turn, stirring after each addition. Turn out on to a plate and serve with the lettuce leaves as a side dish.

potato salad ah-loo thoke

450g (1lb) small new potatoes, boiled and halved (there is no need to peel them)
1 onion, thinly sliced
1 heaped tablespoon crisp-fried shallots (see page 23), to garnish
1 level tablespoon chopped mint leaves, to garnish

for the dressing
2 tablespoons tamarind water (see page 25)
2 tablespoons fish sauce
2 tablespoons groundnut oil
2 teaspoons sugar
3 small red or green chillies, finely chopped

1 Place the boiled new potatoes and the onion in a serving bowl and set aside.

2 In another bowl, prepare the dressing: mix all the ingredients until the sugar has dissolved.

3 Pour the dressing over the potatoes and onions. Mix well, garnish with shallots and mint and serve.

pork and cucumber salad

wetha thakwather thoke

This dish is best prepared in stages, starting about 6 hours before you plan to eat.

1 cucumber, halved, deseeded and cut across into 5mm (¼ in)
   crescents
about 1 litre (1¾ pints) white vinegar
1 level tablespoon sugar
150g (5oz) pork fillet

for the dressing
2 teaspoons groundnut oil
1 tablespoon ground dried shrimp (see page 23)
2 level teaspoons dry-fried sesame seeds (see page 23)
2 level tablespoons crisp-fried shallots (see page 23)

1 Arrange the cucumber crescents in a shallow dish and pour over sufficient vinegar to cover. Sprinkle with sugar and stir to mix.

2 Ensuring that all the cucumber pieces are covered with the liquid, leave to marinate for 5 – 6 hours.

3 Bring a pan of water to the boil, add the pork and simmer for 10 minutes, or until the pork is just cooked through. Remove and, when cool enough to handle, slice thinly. Set aside.

4 When ready to serve, remove the cucumber from the marinade and place in a mixing bowl. Add the pork slices and mix well.

5 Add all the dressing ingredients and mix well. Turn out on a platter and serve.

prawn salad
pazun thoke

My friend Cherie Aung-Khin is an energetic Burmese businesswoman who divides her time between Bangkok – where she sells antiques and craftwork, especially the beautiful lacquerware for which her country is famous – and Rangoon – where she runs the Green Elephant Restaurant in Thirimingalar Lane. There you can find this delicious but ridiculously simple dish, which is also on her menu at the River View Restaurant beside the River Irrawaddy, the famous 'road to Mandalay', in the ancient city of Pagan. According to Khin, this is usually eaten almost as a garnish, with other dishes, but you could eat it on its own if you served it with some salad leaves of your choice.

1 large onion, thinly sliced
10 raw prawns, shelled and deveined
1 heaped tablespoon finely chopped coriander
2 small red or green chillies, finely chopped
1 lime
salt to taste

1 Place the onion on a serving plate and set aside.

2 Bring a pan of water to the boil and briefly dunk the prawns in it until they just change colour. Drain well and place on top of the onions.

3 Sprinkle the coriander and chilli over the prawns, then halve the lime and squeeze the juice of both halves over the prawns. Sprinkle a little salt to taste, mix well and serve.

mango salad
thayethee thoke

1 green (unripe) mango, peeled and grated into long thin strips
1 level tablespoon crisp-fried garlic (see page 23), to garnish

for the dressing
3 small red or green chillies
1 teaspoon shrimp paste
1 teaspoon tamarind water (see page 25)
1 tablespoon fish sauce
1 level tablespoon ground dried shrimp (see page 23)
1 level tablespoon ground roast peanuts
2 level teaspoons dry-fried sesame seeds (see page 23)

1 Place the mango strips in a serving bowl and set aside.

2 Prepare the dressing: preheat a hot grill. Wrap the shrimp paste in foil and grill the parcel for 1 minute on each side. In another bowl, mix together the shrimp paste and all the remaining dressing ingredients.

3 Pour the dressing over the mango and mix well. Garnish with crisp-fried garlic and serve.

bean salad pe-ther thoke

½ teaspoon salt

zest of 1 small lime

225g (8oz) French beans, halved

for the dressing

2 small red shallots

2 garlic cloves

2 small chillies

1 tablespoon sweet soy sauce

2 tablespoons lime juice

1 teaspoon sugar

salt to taste

1 tablespoon groundnut oil

1 tablespoon finely chopped coriander

1 Bring a pan of water to the boil. Add the salt and lime zest. When the water returns to the boil, add the beans and simmer for 5 minutes only. Remove, drain well and arrange on a serving platter. Set aside.

2 Prepare the dressing: in a mortar, pound the shallots, garlic and chillies to a paste. Add the soy sauce, lime juice, sugar and salt. Mix well and pour over the beans.

3 Sprinkle with the oil, then with the chopped coriander and serve.

fish salad nga thoke

225g (8oz) fresh tuna (or similar meaty fish), any skin and bones
   removed

¼ teaspoon salt

1 heaped teaspoon finely chopped turmeric (see page 22)

1 small young lemon grass stalk, chopped into very thin rounds

1 small onion, roughly chopped

1 tablespoon roughly chopped coriander leaf

½ teaspoon chilli powder

1 tablespoon fish sauce

1 tablespoon lime juice

1 level tablespoon crisp-fried shallots (see page 23)

1 level tablespoon crisp-fried garlic (see page 23)

crisp salad, to serve

1 Bring a little water to the boil in a saucepan, add the tuna and simmer briefly until just cooked through. Remove, place in a bowl and break up with a fork.

2 Add all the remaining ingredients and mix well. Turn out on to a plate and serve with a selection of crispy salad leaves.

burmese salad thoke

The Burmese just call this 'salad', but no one has yet been able to tell me why. Though, given the variety of ingredients, it could be seen as the ultimate salad recipe. I've dubbed it 'Burmese salad' just to identify it.

100g (4oz) white cabbage, finely shredded

100g (4oz) carrots, finely shredded

100g (4oz) cucumber, finely shredded

60g (2oz) beansprouts

2 tablespoons oil

4 garlic cloves, thinly sliced

6 small red shallots, thinly sliced

½ teaspoon ground turmeric (see page 22)

½ teaspoon chilli powder

½ teaspoon salt

2 tablespoons lime juice

1 Arrange all the vegetables in a bowl and set aside.

2 Heat the oil in a wok or frying pan and fry the garlic until crisp and golden-brown. Remove, draining well, and add to the bowl.

3 Fry the shallots in the same way and add to the bowl.

4 Add all the remaining ingredients to the bowl and mix well. Turn out on to a platter and serve.

chicken liver salad kyet-athar thoke

225g (8oz) chicken livers, roughly chopped

2 tablespoons fish sauce

1 teaspoon sugar

½ teaspoon chilli powder

1 shallot, finely chopped

2 large spring onions, thinly sliced into rounds

2 tablespoons lemon juice

1 level tablespoon chopped mint leaves

crisp salad, to serve

1 Put 3 tablespoons of water in a saucepan, add the chicken livers and bring to the boil. Reduce the heat and simmer until the livers are just cooked.

2 Remove the pan from the heat, add all remaining ingredients and stir well. Turn out on to a serving dish and serve accompanied by the crisp salad.

grilled prawn and bamboo shoot salad hmyit thoke

10 large raw prawns

150 g (5oz) bamboo shoots, thinly sliced

2 tablespoons coconut cream, to garnish

coriander leaves, to garnish

for the dressing

2 tablespoons fish sauce

2 tablespoons lime juice

2 teaspoons sugar

3 small red or green chillies, finely chopped

1 Preheat the grill to hot and grill the prawns in their shells until they just change colour. When cool enough to handle, peel and devein them. Place the prawns on a serving bowl and set aside.

2 Bring a pan of water to the boil and briefly blanch the bamboo shoots, remove and drain well, then add to the bowl with the prawns.

3 Add all the dressing ingredients to the bowl and stir well. Garnish with coconut cream and a few coriander leaves and serve.

carrot salad au-war-thoke

A Burmese friend tells me that this is more commonly made with white radish (mooli) than carrots and is then called *mane-lar-au-thoke*. Carrots are easier to find, of course, but if you come across white radish then do give it a try, using the same amounts. Mooli has got what the Chinese call a 'cool' taste, which helps counterbalance any spicy flavours.

450g (1lb) young carrots

½ teaspoon salt

1 tablespoon groundnut oil

1 heaped tablespoon black mustard seeds (see page 00)

1 tablespoon lime juice

1 teaspoon sugar

1 Roughly grate the carrots into a bowl and sprinkle with salt. Stir well and leave for 1 hour.

2 Heat the oil in a wok or frying pan and fry the mustard seeds until they begin to jump. Remove and leave to cool.

3 In a small bowl, mix the lime juice and sugar. Stir until the sugar dissolves. Pour over the carrots and stir well. Garnish with the mustard seeds.

spicy fruit salad thit-thu sone thoke

½ **pineapple**

1 **under-ripe mango (not raw but still quite hard)**

½ **pomelo (if necessary, substitute 1 whole grapefruit)**

4 **rose apples (see page 122, if necessary, substitute 2 ordinary apples)**

2 **teaspoons sugar**

¼ **teaspoon chilli powder**

¼ **teaspoon salt**

1 Peel and core the pineapple and cut the flesh into segments. Peel the mango and cut the flesh away from the stone in largish cubes. Peel the pomelo and break it into segments. Halve, stone and core the rose apples, then cut them into pieces about 2.5cm (1in) square.

2 Place all these fruits and the remaining ingredients in a bowl, mix well and serve.

'Nonya, the cuisine that resulted from the inter-marriage of later Chinese immigrants with local women in Malaysia and Indonesia, combines the speed and freshness of Chinese cooking with the richer spices of Southeast Asia. As the Nonya themselves become increasingly integrated into the host society, so their food becomes rarer, though it can still be found in surviving communities on the islands of Penang and Singapore and is well worth searching out for its unique range of tastes.'

malaysia/singapore

Muslim women praying

crispy seaweed gai sung

Despite the fact that it is a clear-cut fraud, crispy seaweed remains eternally popular in Chinese restaurants everywhere. I suppose there must be some people somewhere who have still not sussed out that, far from being an exotic product of the oceans, the so-called 'seaweed' is nothing more than carefully disguised cabbage. The main ingredient is spring greens, that curious leafy vegetable which is really a variety of cabbage that does not develop a heart. More to the point, it is very, very cheap, which is why restaurants love serving it. It is certainly an adaptable dish that can be served on its own as a light starter, or used as stunning decoration on a seafood platter. Perhaps most importantly of all, it is exceptionally easy to make.

450g (1lb) spring greens

10 – 20 dried shrimp (they come in varying sizes, you'll need 10 if large,
   15 if medium and 20 if small)

vegetable oil for deep-frying

½ teaspoon salt

1 teaspoon sugar

1 Cut any hard stalks from the centre of the spring green leaves. Stack the leaves on top of each other and roll into a tight 'cigar'. Thinly slice the leaves into very fine shreds. Spread these out to dry.

2 In a mortar, finely pound the dried shrimp. You will need about 1 heaped tablespoon. Set aside.

3 Heat the oil to quite hot and deep-fry the shredded spring greens a handful at a time (you'll probably need about 4 batches). As soon as they are crisp, remove them with a slotted spoon and drain on kitchen paper.

4 Place on a dish, sprinkle with salt, sugar and the ground shrimp. Stir well and serve.

new year salad yu sheng

As the name implies, this salad is eaten at New Year – Chinese, of course – as fish brings good luck and prosperity. If you don't want to eat unadorned raw fish you could substitute smoked salmon. The preserved ingredients are available in Chinese stores; you will only need a small amount, but the remainder will keep for a long time.

for the garlic oil

3 tablespoons cooking oil

3 garlic cloves, thinly sliced

for the fish

100g (4oz) salmon fillet or smoked salmon, thinly sliced

5cm (2in) piece of young ginger, peeled and finely shredded

½ teaspoon ground white pepper

1 tablespoon lime juice

for the sauce

1 tablespoon sesame oil

5 tablespoons dry sherry

2 tablespoons plum sauce

for the salad

1 carrot, cut into matchsticks

1 white radish (mooli), cut into matchsticks

60g (2oz) preserved sweet papaya

30g (1oz) preserved ginger, thinly sliced

85g (3oz) pomelo segments (you could use grapefruit), torn into shreds

5 kaffir lime leaves, thinly sliced

for the garnish

3 tablespoons ground peanuts

1 teaspoon five-spice powder

1 tablespoon dry-fried sesame seeds (see page 23)

1 First make the garlic oil: heat the oil in a wok or frying pan and fry the garlic slices until golden-brown, then set aside in the oil.

2 Prepare the fish: in a bowl, mix the fish with 1 tablespoon of the garlic oil with its garlic. Add the ginger, pepper and lime juice. Mix and set aside.

3 Make the sauce: place the remaining 2 tablespoons of garlic oil in a bowl, add all the remaining sauce ingredients, mix well and set aside.

4 Prepare the salad: mix all the ingredients in a bowl, add the fish, pour over the sauce and mix well.

5 Sprinkle over the garnish ingredients and serve.

avocado salad makhan chaat

This recipe reflects the Indian influence on Malaysian and Singaporean cuisine. Normally, milk-based products like cheese and yoghurt are unknown in Southeast Asian food, but here they are principal ingredients in this refreshing dish.

2 large, just ripe, avocado pears
a squeeze of lemon juice
100g (4oz) cottage cheese
5 chive stalks, finely chopped
5 tablespoons plain natural yoghurt
1 garlic clove, crushed
2 green chillies, finely chopped
salt and pepper
4 medium lettuce leaves, shredded (a variety of different leaves, such as frisée, radicchio, etc., would look good)
paprika and mint leaves, to garnish

1 Cut around the middle of the avocados lengthwise down to the stone and carefully separate the two halves. Remove the stones and scoop out the flesh with a spoon, while preserving the outer shells. Rub the insides of the avocado shells with lemon juice and set aside. Cut the flesh into small cubes, about 1cm (1/2 inch).

2 In a bowl, mix the cottage cheese and chopped chives. Add the yoghurt, garlic and chillies, with salt and pepper to taste. Mix well and carefully fold in the avocado cubes. Chill in the refrigerator.

3 Line the insides of each of the avocado shell with some of the shredded lettuce leaves. Place some of the chilled avocado mixture in each and garnish with a sprinkling of paprika and a little shredded mint leaf. Serve immediately.

Illuminated statue of the Merlion, the 'Lion of the Sea', heraldic symbol of the Island Republic, on Clifford Pier, Singapore

chicken salad with sesame dressing

bon bon ji

2 skinless chicken breast fillets

1 whole small head of Chinese celery (or substitute a large head of Western celery)

1 tablespoon sesame oil

3 spring onions, thinly sliced, to garnish

for the dressing

2 tablespoons light soy sauce

1 teaspoon sugar

1 teaspoon chilli oil

1 heaped teaspoon sesame seeds

1 Bring a pan of water to the boil, add the chicken and simmer until just cooked through, about 8 minutes. When cool enough to handle, remove and shred into a bowl with your hands.

2 Break up the celery, discarding any hard outer pieces. Cut off the broad hard section near the base of each piece to leave a stem of equal width, top and bottom. Pull away any leaves at the top and set these aside. Chop the celery into thin matchsticks.

3 Place the chopped celery, the reserved leaves and the shredded chicken in a bowl, cover with sesame oil, stir well and set aside.

4 Make the dressing by mixing all the ingredients in a small bowl and set aside.

5 Pour the dressing over the chicken and celery mixture. Stir well and turn out on to a serving plate. Garnish with the spring onion and serve.

sweet-and-sour cucumber salad

tan chu huang gua

1 slender cucumber, about 30cm (12in) long

1 teaspoon salt

2 teaspoons sugar

1 tablespoon rice vinegar

1 teaspoon chilli oil

1 tablespoon sesame oil

1 At least 30 minutes before you want to serve, halve the unpeeled cucumber lengthwise. Scrape out the seeds and cut the halves across into thick chunks.

2 Place the cucumber pieces in a bowl and sprinkle with salt. Mix well and leave for 30 minutes.

3 At the end of this time, add the sugar, vinegar and chilli oil. Mix well.

4 Just before serving, sprinkle with the sesame oil.

hot and sour cabbage salad

suan la pai cai

450g (1lb) white cabbage

2 tablespoons vegetable oil

2 large dried red chillies, roughly chopped

1 teaspoon salt

1 tablespoon brown sugar

1 tablespoon light soy sauce

2 tablespoons rice vinegar

1 teaspoon sesame oil

1 Cut the cabbage leaves into small pieces about 2.5x1cm (1x½in)

2 Heat the oil in a wok or frying pan and fry the chillies briefly. Add the cabbage and stir-fry for 2 minutes. Add the salt and sugar, and stir-fry for 1 minute more.

3 Add the soy sauce, vinegar and sesame oil. Quickly stir well, then turn out on to a dish and serve.

egg pancake salad

nonya popiab

This is an unusual dish in that pancakes are stuffed with salad and also served with it as an accompaniment, making a substantial one-dish meal.

for the salad

6 large lettuce leaves

60g (2oz) beansprouts

for the filling

2 tablespoons vegetable oil

1 teaspoon finely chopped ginger

1 large garlic clove, finely chopped

2 small red chillies, finely chopped

1 tablespoon white wine vinegar

2 teaspoons sugar

100g (4oz) white radish (mooli), grated

1 carrot, grated

100g (4oz) white cabbage, shredded

1 red onion, quartered and then thinly sliced

for the pancakes

2 eggs

½ teaspoon salt

100g (4oz) plain flour

1 tablespoon vegetable oil

1 Arrange the lettuce leaves and beansprouts on a serving dish and set aside.

2 Make the filling: heat the oil in a frying pan or wok, add the ginger, garlic and chillies and gently fry until the garlic is golden brown. Add the remaining filling ingredients, stir-fry for 3 – 4 minutes until the vegetables begin to soften, and set aside.

3 Make the pancakes: break the eggs into a bowl, whisk and then stir in the salt. Add the flour, little by little and stirring constantly until smooth. Then add 150 ml (¼ pint) of water, a little at a time, mixing well.

4 Heat half the oil in a large frying pan and, when hot, add half the egg batter and cook until the underside browns. Toss and brown the other side. Turn out on to a plate and repeat the process to make a second pancake.

5 Fill each pancake with half the prepared vegetable mix and roll into a tube. Set these among the reserved salad and serve.

tomato salad
tamatar kasondi

2 limes
1/2 teaspoon sugar
salt and ground black pepper
2 onions, finely chopped
5 firm tomatoes, finely chopped
1 large green chilli, finely chopped
10 coriander leaves
10 mint leaves, to garnish

1 Squeeze the juice from the limes into a bowl. Add the sugar with salt and pepper to taste. Set aside until the sugar and salt dissolve.

2 Add the onions, tomatoes, chillies and coriander leaves. Mix well.

3 Garnish with mint leaves and serve.

fried beancurd, cucumber and beansprouts with spicy peanut sauce
tahu goring

oil for deep-frying
4 blocks of beancurd (tofu), each about 5cm (2in) square
100g (4oz) beansprouts
1 cucumber, thinly sliced

for the dressing
2 large garlic cloves
3-4 small red chillies
1 tablespoon vegetable oil
1 tablespoon tamarind water (see page 25)
1 tablespoon dark soy sauce
1 tablespoon light soy sauce
6 tablespoons water
1 tablespoon sugar
salt (about 1/4 teaspoon)
150g (5oz) ground roast peanuts

1 Heat the oil for deep-frying until very hot and deep-fry the beancurd blocks until golden-brown. Drain on kitchen paper and, when cool enough to handle, cut each block in half, then slice each half into 8 strips and set aside.

2 Tail the beansprouts and place in a salad bowl. Add the cucumber to the bowl and mix with the beansprouts. Place the beancurd strips on top and set aside.

3 Prepare the dressing: in a mortar, pound together the garlic and chillies to a paste. Heat the oil in a wok or frying pan, add the paste and stir well. Then add all the remaining dressing ingredients in turn, stirring after each. Finally stir in the peanuts well until a sauce forms.

4 Pour the sauce into a sauce bowl and serve alongside the salad.

beansprouts with spicy prawn salad
kerabu taugeh

Nonya, the cuisine that resulted from the intermarriage of later Chinese immigrants with local women in Malaysia and Indonesia, combines the speed and freshness of Chinese cooking with the richer spices of Southeast Asia. As the Nonya themselves become increasingly integrated into the host society, so their food becomes rarer, though it can still be found in surviving communities on the islands of Penang and Singapore and is well worth searching out for its unique range of tastes.

For this dish you need a mature coconut with a hard brown shell and solid white coconut flesh inside – not the young green coconut with soft milky flesh most commonly found in Asia. As the hard brown variety is usually all one can find in the West, for once overseas cooks have an advantage over the locals. You will probably have to buy a whole coconut, even though only a small amount is required for this recipe. The rest could be used for cakes or eaten on its own as a nut.

225g (8oz) beansprouts
1 large red onion, quartered and thinly sliced
60g (2oz) hard white coconut (see above)
30g (1oz) dried shrimp (see page 23)
1 tablespoon vegetable oil
1 teaspoon shrimp paste (see page 24)
2-3 small red chillies, finely chopped
150g (5oz) raw prawns, peeled and deveined
1 lime

Restoring the old in the midst of the new in Kuala Lumpur

1 Tail the beansprouts and place in a salad bowl with the onion.

2 Crack open the coconut. Take a piece and pull away the shell. You will be left with solid white coconut about 1 cm (½in) thick. Very thinly slice the coconut, first into little squares and then again until you have tiny pieces the size of rice grains.

3 Dry-fry the coconut grains until golden brown and crisp. Add to the salad bowl.

4 In a mortar, pound the dried shrimp to a coarse powder and add to the salad bowl. Mix the salad ingredients well and set aside.

5 Heat the oil in a wok or frying pan and stir-fry the shrimp paste until it breaks up in the oil. Add the chillies and prawns and stir-fry for roughly 2 minutes, until the prawns are just cooked through. Remove from the heat.

6 Turn out on to the salad, squeeze in the juice of the lime, stir well and serve.

green salad with coconut and mint dressing syabas

100g (4oz) mange tout, topped, tailed and halved

100g (4oz) French beans, trimmed and halved

1 small cucumber, halved lengthwise, deseeded and cut into pieces 5cm (2in) long

100g (4oz) Chinese cabbage, roughly shredded

100g (4oz) broccoli, stems cut away to leave small florets

for the dressing

2 tablespoons vegetable oil

1 large garlic clove, crushed

2 small green chillies, finely chopped

2 teaspoons sugar

3 tablespoons coconut cream

1 tablespoon fish sauce

2 tablespoons lime juice

1 tablespoons finely chopped mint leaves

1 Bring a pan of water to the boil and one by one blanch each type of vegetable in turn for 4 minutes, refreshing each in cold water and draining them well. Place all the vegetables in a large bowl and set aside.

2 Prepare the dressing: heat the oil in a saucepan and fry the garlic until golden-brown. Add all the other dressing ingredients, except the lime juice and mint, together with 5 tablespoons of water and stir well. Remove from the heat and stir in the lime juice and mint.

3 Pour the dressing over the reserved vegetables, stir well and serve.

pineapple pickle with grilled prawn salad acar nanas

1 crispy lettuce, such as Cos
450g (1lb) raw prawns

for the pickle
1 teaspoon fennel seeds
1 teaspoon cumin seeds
1 teaspoon coriander seeds
2 large dried chillies, soaked in warm water for 10 minutes
8 small shallots
5 garlic cloves
2 tablespoons cooking oil
3 cloves
3 star anise
1 cinnamon stick
1 small pineapple, peeled, cored and cut into segments
3 curry leaves
3 large green chillies
1 tablespoon sugar
salt

1 First make the pineapple pickle: in a mortar, pound together the seeds, chillies, shallots and garlic to a paste and set aside.

2 In a wok or frying pan, heat the oil and fry the paste, stirring well. Add the cloves, star anise and cinnamon, and stir well. Add the pineapple segments, curry leaves, chillies, sugar and salt to taste, and stir well. Lower the heat and simmer for 30 minutes, until the consistency is that of a thick chutney.

3 Arrange the lettuce leaves on a platter and set aside.

4 Preheat a hot grill and grill the prawns until they change colour, about 2 minutes on each side. When cool enough to handle, remove the shells and place the prawns on the salad.

5 Spread the pickle on the prawn and salad (the exact amount will depend on the quantity of lettuce) and serve.

fruit and vegetable salad with shrimp paste dressing rojak

1 small green mango, peeled and sliced
1 small pineapple, peeled, cored and cut into segments
1 cucumber, thinly sliced
1 large carrot, sliced into fine matchsticks

for the dressing
1 teaspoon shrimp paste (see page 24)
2 large garlic cloves
2 or 3 small red chillies
1 tablespoon tamarind water (see page 25)
1 tablespoon sugar
salt

1 Arrange the salad ingredients in a bowl and set aside.

2 Make the dressing: preheat a hot grill. Wrap the shrimp paste in foil and grill the foil parcel for 1 minute on each side. In a mortar, pound the grilled shrimp paste with all the other ingredients to a paste .

3 Add the paste to the salad and mix well. Serve.

fruit and yoghurt salad mava raitha

This is a version of the Indian raitha, although instead of being served as a soothing milky side dish for a curry it has grown into a fully fledged dessert with Indian flavours.

1 small pot of plain yoghurt
85g (3oz) green seedless grapes, halved
2 medium bananas, peeled and sliced
60g (2oz) walnuts, roughly pounded
2 teaspoons sugar
1 teaspoon ground cumin
salt
paprika, to garnish

1 Place the yoghurt in a bowl and mix in all the remaining ingredients with salt to taste.

2 Sprinkle with paprika and serve.

banana flower and dried shrimp and sambal salad jantung pisang kerabu

This can be served on its own or, as the flavour is quite strong, with an undressed lettuce salad; I prefer the extra leaves. If you can't find a banana flower, use endive (chicory) which should not be boiled as it is sufficiently tender.

2 tablespoons cooking oil
1 tablespoon tamarind water (see page 25)
1 tablespoon sugar
salt
2 tablespoons grated coconut
1 banana flower (see page 19, prepared as described)
lime juice, freshly squeezed

for the sambal dressing
1 tablespoon dried shrimp
2 large dried chillies, soaked in warm water for 10 minutes
1 young lemon grass stalk, any hard outer layer discarded and thinly sliced
4 small shallots
2 large garlic cloves

1 Make the sambal dressing: in a mortar, pound the dried shrimp, chillies, lemon grass, shallots and garlic to a paste and set aside.

2 In a wok or frying pan, heat 1 tablespoon of the oil and add the reserved sambal paste, stirring constantly. Add the tamarind water, sugar and salt to taste, stirring until the sugar and salt have dissolved. Transfer to a small bowl.

3 Heat the remaining oil, turn the heat to low, add the coconut and brown it. When crisp, remove and set aside.

4 Place the banana flower, sambal sauce and fried coconut in a bowl. Add lime juice to taste, mix well and serve.

indonesia

'Most tourists do no more than cast a passing glance at the beautifully composed stacks of fruit and vegetables but, with this book in mind, I was having a good rummage round a stall piled high with tight crisp lettuces and huge sprays of a plant I'd never seen before, when I uncovered some sheets of newspaper stained with very rich colours. I flicked them over and uncovered a set of beautiful close-up portraits of Balinese men and women in traditional head-dresses in a style that seemed to bring together delicate Oriental stylization with the power of Western realism. As I stood admiring the little pictures I was suddenly aware of being watched – by the stall-holder, who was also the artist, clearly nervous about my reaction to his work.'

Classic *Wayang Galek* puppet performance

mixed salad with peanut dressing
gado gado

After sate, this is probably the best-known Indonesian dish. Even those who have tried it, though, may be unaware of how much it varies from place to place and cook to cook. A meal in itself, gado gado can be made with a range of raw or partly cooked ingredients, the one constant being the peanut sauce dressing, but even here there is room for variation. Being Thai, I've chosen a noticeably spicy example, which I think goes well with the blandness of the egg, beancurd and potato. You can adjust ingredients like chilli, adding more or less as you prefer – every Indonesian has his or her preference, so feel free.

2 hard-boiled eggs
85g (3oz) long beans, cut into 2.5cm (1in) lengths
85g (3oz) cauliflower, roughly chopped
85g (3oz) carrot, roughly cut into small cubes
85g (3oz) beansprouts
oil for deep-frying
85g (3oz) beancurd (tofu), cut into 2.5cm (1in) cubes
1 potato, cut into small cubes

for the dressing
2 tablespoons oil
2 large garlic cloves, finely chopped
2 shallots, finely chopped
4 tablespoons coconut cream
2 tablespoons fish sauce
1 tablespoon tamarind water (see page 25)
2 teaspoons sugar
½ teaspoon chilli powder
3 tablespoons ground roast peanuts

1 Shell the eggs, cut the eggs into quarters and set aside. Bring a pan of water to the boil. Add the long beans, cauliflower, carrot and beansprouts and blanch for 3 minutes. Remove, drain on kitchen paper and set aside to cool.

2 Heat the oil to medium-hot, add the beancurd and fry until golden-brown. Remove, drain on kitchen paper and set aside.

3 Add the potato cubes to the hot oil and fry until golden brown. Remove, drain on kitchen paper and set aside.

4 When the blanched vegetables are cool, arrange them in a serving bowl, add the deep-fried beancurd and potato and top with the egg quarters. Set aside.

5 Make the dressing: heat the oil to quite hot and fry the garlic and shallots until golden-brown. Add all the remaining ingredients in turn, stirring after each addition. When they are all stirred in, simmer and stir for 30 seconds, until the sauce blends and thickens. Remove from the heat and allow to cool briefly.

6 Pour over the salad and serve.

spicy chicken salad with ginger
ayam selada

This is really a starter, but would also make a rather unusual canapé.

2 skinless chicken breast fillets

1 teaspoon finely chopped ginger

1 onion, cut into small cubes

1 red pepper, deseeded and cut into small cubes

3 spring onions, roughly chopped

8 Cos lettuce leaves, to serve

for the dressing

1 large garlic clove, finely chopped

2 small red or green chillies, finely chopped

2 tablespoons fish sauce

2 tablespoons lime juice

2 tablespoons sugar

1 Bring a pan of water to the boil, add the chicken and simmer until just cooked through, about 10 minutes. When cool enough to handle, remove and, using the fingers, shred into a large serving bowl.

2 Add the ginger, onion, red pepper and spring onions to the chicken. Mix together well and set aside.

3 Make the dressing by mixing all the ingredients in a small bowl. Pour over the reserved chicken mixture and stir well.

4 Serve the dressed mixture in its bowl with the lettuce leaves on a serving dish. Diners should spoon a little of the mixture on to a leaf, fold it up around the filling, then eat it like a sandwich.

cooked vegetable salad in a coconut and tamarind sauce lawar

1 large potato, cut into small cubes, about 1cm (½in)

85g (3oz) long beans, cut to 2.5cm (1in) lengths

85g (3oz) beansprouts

85g (3oz) sweetcorn kernels

for the dressing

2 large garlic cloves

2-3 small red chillies

1 tablespoon oil

4 tablespoons coconut cream (see page 23)

2 tablespoons fish sauce

1 tablespoons sugar

1 tablespoon tamarind water (see page 25)

for the garnish

1 large red chilli, thinly sliced into rounds

1 heaped tablespoon crisp-fried shallot (see page 23)

1 Bring 2 large pans of water to the boil. Add the potato cubes to one and simmer for 10 minutes. While the potatoes are cooking, one by one blanch the long beans, beansprouts and sweetcorn in the other pan for 30 seconds each. Drain each well and place in a large bowl. Finally, drain the potato cubes and add to the bowl.

2 Prepare the dressing: in a mortar, pound the garlic and chillies together to a paste. Heat the oil in a wok or frying pan and fry the paste, stirring well. Add the remaining ingredients together with 2 tablespoons of water, stirring well.

3 Pour the dressing over the salad and mix well. Garnish with chilli and crisp-fried shallot to serve.

grilled beef salad
getchok

As the arts and crafts centre of central Bali, it is appropriate that the little town of Ubud should have a number of resort hotels built in traditional style that try to recapture something of the atmosphere of a classic island village – temple forecourts and palace corridors, the shady passageways between high stone walls that suddenly open on to a panorama of terraced rice fields and distant mountains. Perhaps the best of these is the Amandari, built on a hillside just outside of town, with a sensational view across a wide green valley. The place to enjoy this at its best is the main restaurant in a raised stilt house, which offers a traditional Balinese feast that I just had to try. When they heard about this book, the chefs there were happy to see that among the many dishes there were special local salads, which I have tried to record in this and the *lawar* opposite. Though I can't bring you the view, I can possibly help you resurrect some of the flavours.

Beancurd and tempe

1 cucumber, thinly sliced

1 onion, cut into thin wedges

2 large tomatoes, cut into thin wedges

225g (8oz) fillet steak

for the dressing

2 tablespoons fish sauce

2 tablespoons lime juice

2 small red chillies, finely chopped

2 teaspoons sugar

for the garnish

1 heaped tablespoon finely chopped mint leaves

1 heaped tablespoon crisp-fried shallot (see page 23)

1 Preheat a hot grill. Arrange the cucumber, onion and tomato in a salad bowl and set aside.

2 Make the dressing by mixing together all the ingredients in a small bowl, stirring until the sugar is dissolved. Set aside.

3 Grill the steak to taste (about 3 – 5 minutes on each side for medium-rare). When cool enough to handle, slice it thinly into bite-sized pieces, being sure to reserve any juices.

4 Place the steak on the salad with any juices, add the dressing and stir well.

5 Garnish with mint leaves and shallot and serve.

duck with tempe ihk suir utck-utck

Tempe is a soya bean cake filled with yellow beans, adding an agreeably savoury edge and crunchy texture to an otherwise rather bland substance. Tempe is much used in Indonesian cooking, but it is always made in large quantities and bought ready-made in food markets. I was going to say that I had never seen it outside Indonesia but, just as this book was about to go to press, I came across a packet in a London specialist organic store. What I've done here is provide a recipe for those few who manage to find some real tempe, together with an alternative that will give something of the flavour and texture of the original.

2 duck breasts
oil for deep-frying
1 packet of tempe (the one I found was 10cm (4in) square by (1cm)
 ¹⁄₂in thick), halved and then cut into slices about 5cm (2in) by
 1cm (¹⁄₂in), or 2 blocks of fresh beancurd (tofu), cut into small
 cubes about 1 cm (¹⁄₂in)
2 tablespoons ground roast peanuts (if using the beancurd)
4 kaffir lime leaves
100g (4oz) beansprouts
1 large red sweet pepper, deseeded and sliced into fine matchsticks
4 spring onions, thinly sliced
2 limes
salt

for the marinade
2 garlic cloves
¹⁄₂ teaspoon black peppercorns
¹⁄₂ teaspoon coriander seeds
¹⁄₂ teaspoon salt
2 teaspoons sugar

1 First make the marinade: in a mortar, pound the garlic, peppercorns and coriander seeds together to a paste.

2 Spread the paste over the duck breasts, covering them well. Sprinkle with salt and sugar and leave to marinate.

3 Heat the oil for deep-frying until it is very hot but not sizzling and fry the tempe or beancurd until crisp and golden. Remove from the oil, draining well, and transfer to a bowl. Keep the oil hot. If using the beancurd, add the ground peanuts to the bowl.

4 Pile the kaffir lime leaves on top of each other, roll up tightly into a 'cigarette' and sliced this across to make fine strips. Put these in a fine strainer and quickly dip the kaffir lime leaf shreds in and out of the hot oil; they will instantly become crisp. Drain well, place in the bowl with the fried tempe or beancurd and set aside.

5 Preheat a hot grill. Arrange the beansprouts, pepper strips and spring onions in a bowl and set aside.

6 Grill the marinated duck to taste (see page 39). When the duck is cool enough to handle, cut it into thin slices.

7 Place the duck slices on the salad, add the tempe or beancurd and peanuts and the kaffir lime leaf. Add lime juice and salt to taste and serve.

water spinach with prawn salad
pelecing kangkung

225g (8oz) water spinach (morning glory)
175g (6oz) raw prawns, shelled and deveined

for the dressing
2 large garlic cloves
4 small red shallots
2 large dried chillies, soaked in warm water for 10 minutes, then drained
  and roughly chopped
2 tablespoons cooking oil
4 tablespoons coconut cream
2 tablespoons sugar
2 tablespoons fish sauce
2 tablespoons lime juice
2 tablespoons ground roast peanuts

1 Bring a large pan of water to the boil. Remove all the leaves from the water spinach and set aside. Chop the stems into 5mm (¼in) pieces and blanch these for 30 seconds only, then blanch the leaves for a brief second. Drain both well, place on a serving dish and set aside.

2 Dip the prawns briefly in the same boiling water just until they change colour. Drain, place on the salad and set aside.

3 Prepare the dressing: in a mortar, pound together the garlic, shallots and chillies to a paste. Heat the oil in a frying pan or wok and briefly stir-fry the chilli paste. Add the coconut cream, mix well with the paste and then add all the remaining ingredients in turn, stirring after each.

4 Pour the dressing over the prawns and salad to serve.

cucumber and beansprout salad
dabu dabu kenari

225g (8oz) cucumber, peeled and sliced
225g (8oz) beansprouts
4 small shallots, thinly sliced
10 sweet basil leaves

for the dressing
½ teaspoon shrimp paste
3 tablespoons lime juice
2 tablespoons hot water
2 teaspoons sugar
½ teaspoon salt
4 small red and green chillies, finely chopped

1 Arrange the cucumber, beansprouts and shallots in a bowl and set aside.

2 Prepare the dressing: preheat a hot grill, wrap the shrimp paste in foil and grill the parcel for 1 minute on each side. In another bowl, mix the grilled shrimp paste with all the remaining dressing ingredients and stir until the sugar dissolves.

3 Pile the basil leaves on top of each other, roll tightly into a 'cigarette' and slice this across to make thin shreds.

4 Pour the dressing over the salad, mix well, garnish with the basil shreds and serve.

pineapple and shrimp salad

lalab nenas muda

This recipe was inspired by one of the dishes at Ari's Warang in Ubud (see page 14), and could be used as a Western-style starter.

8 raw prawns
8 large lettuce leaves, roughly broken up
1 small sweet red pepper, deseeded and cut into long thin slices
1 pineapple, peeled, cored and cut into segments
1 tablespoon finely chopped chives, to garnish

for the dressing
1 tablespoon sweet soy sauce
2 tablespoons lemon juice
2 teaspoons sugar
3 small red chillies, finely chopped
salt

1 Bring a pan of water to the boil. Peel and devein the prawns, then dip them in the boiling water until they just change colour. Immediately remove and place them briefly in cold water to stop the cooking process. Drain well and set aside.

2 Arrange the lettuce and sweet pepper on a serving dish and set aside.

3 Make the dressing by mixing all the ingredients together in a bowl with salt to taste, stirring until the sugar dissolves. Add the pineapple segments and mix well.

4 Turn the dressing out on to the salad, garnish with chives and serve.

Dawn breaks over the largest Buddhist monument in the world, Borobodur, central Java

Rose apples

fruit and vegetable salad asinan

I went to Java to see Borobodur, the world's largest Buddhist monument. I had a terrific guide who managed to get me into the heavily locked and guarded site before dawn, so that I could climb to the summit of the fabulously sculpted ziggurat and sit alone amongst the monumental Buddhas to watch the sunrise – one of the most moving experiences of my life.

That evening I asked him if we could avoid the usual tourist restaurants and eat somewhere local, so he cleverly drove me to the conventional suburban bungalow of a couple who do a bit of catering from their home. It was just what I wanted. We sat on the veranda next to their kitchen, alternately watching them cook while half-watching television, which is obligatory in Asia. Just as in Thailand, dishes emerged as they were cooked and we drank and nibbled until everything had appeared and our hosts could join us so the serious eating could begin.

This recipe is for one of the more unusual dishes they serve. Treating raw unsweetened fruits as vegetables is common in Asia, but this mix of riper – and thus sweeter – fruit with savoury vegetables is adventurous.

100g (4oz) barely ripe papaya(s)

1 small cucumber

2 star fruit, thinly sliced to make thin stars

100g (4oz) rose apple(s) (you could substitute ordinary apple at a pinch), quartered then thinly sliced across

2 carrots, sliced into fine matchsticks

100g (4oz) beansprouts, tailed

for the dressing

225ml (8fl oz) white vinegar

4 tablespoons sugar

½ teaspoon salt

2 garlic cloves, finely chopped

4 small red chillies, finely chopped

to garnish

2 tablespoons finely ground dried shrimp (see page 23)

2 tablespoons dry-roasted peanuts

1 Peel the papaya(s), halve and remove the seeds, then cut each half lengthwise into 4 strips. Cut these across into 5mm (¼in) pieces. Peel the cucumber and deseed it, then slice it into thin crescents.

2 Arrange these in a bowl with the remaining fruits and vegetables, and set aside.

3 Prepare the dressing: in another bowl, mix the vinegar and sugar and stir until the sugar dissolves. Add all the remaining dressing ingredients and stir well.

4 Pour the dressing over the salad, mix well and garnish with ground shrimp and peanuts to serve.

fried sweet potato salad
kentang coloh-coloh

After 'doing' Borobodur (see page 122), temple fanatics are supposed to visit a selection of other wonders in the region, so I let my brilliant driver/guide take me to Candi Mendut, a tall structure in whose crepuscular interior a massive Buddha is seated – not in the usual lotus-position but almost like a European, in an upright chair. It is quite unique.

It was lunchtime when we emerged blinking into the sunlight and we quickly crossed to a nearby workers' café where, again unusually for Asia, a sort of quick-service buffet was set out on a heated counter, so you just had to point to get a selection instantly dished up. As this salad was the only fresh thing on offer among all the stews and curry-like dishes, I had to have it and I wasn't disappointed for, while the vegetables make it quite a hefty dish, the dressing is suitably light and refreshing for a midday meal on a very hot day.

450g (1lb) sweet potato, peeled and cut into 1cm (½in) cubes
2 tablespoons groundnut oil
2 tablespoons lemon juice
¼ teaspoon salt
oil for deep-frying
1 green sweet pepper, deseeded and finely diced
1 large tomato, finely diced
1 level tablespoon finely chopped parsley

for the dressing
2 small shallots, finely chopped
2 garlic cloves, finely chopped
4 small red chillies
1 tablespoon sweet soy sauce
1 level tablespoon sugar

1 First prepare the dressing: in a mortar, pound the shallots, garlic and chillies to a paste. Add the soy sauce, sugar and 2 tablespoons of water. Stir until the sugar dissolves and set aside.

2 Place the sweet potato cubes in a shallow bowl. Add the groundnut oil, mix well and then place in the upper compartment of a steamer and steam for 10 minutes. Remove from the heat, add the lemon juice and salt and mix well.

3 Heat the oil for deep-frying and deep-fry the steamed sweet potato until golden-brown. Drain well and place on kitchen pepper to soak up any excess oil.

4 Place the fried sweet potato on a serving platter with the pepper, tomato and parsley. Mix well, add the dressing and stir well again to serve.

javanese salad karedok

This salad can be served with prawn crackers, which can be bought dried with simple instructions for deep-frying. Nowadays some of the ready-made versions available in packets among the potato crisps are also very good.

1 small cucumber, peeled and thinly sliced
85g (3oz) beansprouts
4 small red shallots, thinly sliced
4 small round aubergines (see page 19), thinly sliced
100g (4oz) long beans, cut into 5cm (2in) lengths
100g (4oz) cauliflower, broken into small florets

for the dressing
1 teaspoon shrimp paste
2 large garlic cloves, roughly chopped
4 small red chillies
1 tablespoon tamarind water (see page 25)
1 level tablespoon sugar
2 tablespoons fish sauce
1 tablespoon water

1 First prepare the dressing: preheat a hot grill, wrap the shrimp paste in foil and grill the parcel for 1 minute on each side. In a mortar, pound the garlic and chilli, then add the grilled shrimp paste, stir well and add all the other dressing ingredients, stirring until the sugar is dissolved. Set aside.

2 Arrange the cucumber, beansprouts and shallots on a serving platter.

3 Bring a pan of water to the boil and one by one briefly blanch the aubergines, long beans and cauliflower florets in turn, long enough to be just tender but keeping them firm. Drain well and place on the salad.

4 Cover the salad with the dressing and serve.

spinach salad lalab bayam

225g (8oz) baby spinach leaves
¼ teaspoon salt

for the dressing
2 garlic cloves, finely chopped
3 small red chillies, finely chopped
2 tablespoons lime juice
2 level teaspoons sugar

1 First make the dressing by mixing all the ingredients in a bowl, stirring until the sugar dissolves. Set aside.

2 Remove any thick stalks from the spinach. Bring a pan of water to the boil, add the salt followed by the spinach. As soon as the water returns to the boil, remove the spinach, drain well and transfer to a serving platter.

3 Cover the spinach with the dressing, stir well and serve.

steamed mixed vegetables with spicy coconut dressing jangan olah

I was taken to a local market on Java and was intrigued to see that, instead of the usual food stalls clustered near the entrance – serving noodles and rice dishes – that you find all over Asia, the sides of the main market hall were lined with tiny curtained-off, rather dark rooms in which diners sat discretely eating their meals. They looked like voting booths or somewhere you might go to get your fortune told.

100g (4oz) broccoli
100g (4oz) pumpkin, peeled and cut into 2.5cm (1in) cubes
100g (4oz) potato(es), peeled and cut into 2.5cm (1in) cubes
100g (4oz) French beans, halved.
1 tablespoon crisp-fried shallot (see page 23), to garnish

for the dressing
1 teaspoon shrimp paste
4 garlic cloves, roughly chopped
4 small shallots, roughly chopped
2.5cm (1in) piece of turmeric, peeled and roughly chopped
4 small red chillies, roughly chopped
2 teaspoons palm sugar
225ml (8fl oz) coconut milk
½ teaspoon salt

1 First prepare the dressing: preheat a hot grill, wrap the shrimp paste in foil and grill the parcel for 1 minute on each side. In a mortar, pound the garlic, shallots, turmeric, chillies and grilled shrimp paste, mixing well. Add the palm sugar and mix well again. Add the coconut milk together with an equal volume of water and the salt. Stir well until the sugar and salt dissolves. Set aside.

2 Cut away and discard most of the broccoli's hard stems, leaving only the florets with a short upper stem each.

3 Bring some water to the boil in the lower compartment of a steamer. Place the pumpkin, potatoes, broccoli and beans in the upper compartment and steam for about 15 minutes, or until the vegetables are just tender but still firm.

4 Transfer the vegetables to a serving platter, pour over the dressing (it should first be well mixed at the table), garnish with crisp-fried shallot and serve.

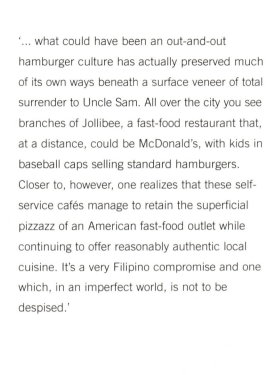

the philippines

'... what could have been an out-and-out hamburger culture has actually preserved much of its own ways beneath a surface veneer of total surrender to Uncle Sam. All over the city you see branches of Jollibee, a fast-food restaurant that, at a distance, could be McDonald's, with kids in baseball caps selling standard hamburgers. Closer to, however, one realizes that these self-service cafés manage to retain the superficial pizzazz of an American fast-food outlet while continuing to offer reasonably authentic local cuisine. It's a very Filipino compromise and one which, in an imperfect world, is not to be despised.'

Slightly surreal waterside sculptural group showing American General MacArthur wading ashore to 'reclaim' the Philippines from the Japanese, at Red Beach, Leyte

banana blossom salad
ensaladang puso ng saging

I came across this and six other salad recipes at the Amanpulo resort on Pamalican island. Pamalican is special because the management and staff are trying to preserve the marine turtles who return to the island thirty years after their birth to lay their first eggs in the sand above sea-level, and who are threatened with extinction across Southeast Asia. For a luxury hotel to take on this task is splendid and if visitors to the island are lucky they can witness one of the nights when the newly hatched baby turtles are released into the water to begin their arduous struggle for survival against many animal predators, the worst of which walks around on two legs!

Nature aside, the great thing about the Amanpulo is the food – these salads were prepared by the head chef, Fritz Zwahlen, and his team. Some were served at the clubhouse by the ocean, others in the elegant poolside dining room, and all bring back very pleasant memories. I am grateful to Fritz for sharing them with me. The other salads from Amanpulo I've adapted here are: Tomato and White Radish Salad (page 132); Roasted Eggplant Salad (page 135); Fresh Tuna Pickled in Lime Juice with Ginger, Chilli, Onion and Sweet Pepper (page 136); Pomelo Salad (page 137); Corn, Sweet Pepper and Crab Meat Salad (page 137); and Jack Fruit Salad (page 138).

6 lettuce leaves

1 banana flower (see page 19, prepared as described)

3 small sweet peppers (one each red, yellow and green), deseeded and finely diced

60g (2 oz) boiled crab meat, to garnish

for the dressing

2 tablespoons white vinegar

2 garlic cloves, finely chopped

2 teaspoons sugar

1 teaspoon olive oil

½ teaspoon salt

¼ teaspoon ground black pepper

1 Arrange the lettuce leaves on a serving platter and set aside.

2 Make the dressing by mixing together all the ingredients in a bowl and set aside.

3 Bring a pan of water to the boil and briefly blanch the banana flower petals. Drain well and place in a bowl. Add the sweet peppers, mix well, then add the dressing and mix well again.

4 Place the dressed salad on top of the lettuce leaves and garnish with crab meat to serve.

tomato and white radish salad ensaladang labanos at kamatis

1 small white radish (mooli), peeled and thinly sliced
½ teaspoon salt
2 large tomatoes, thinly sliced

for the dressing
2 tablespoons white vinegar
2 teaspoons sugar
1 tablespoon light soy sauce
¼ teaspoon ground black pepper

to garnish
1 red chilli, sliced into thin matchsticks
coriander leaves

1 Place the white radish in a bowl, sprinkle with salt and mix well. Briefly squeeze with the fingers to mix and set aside.

2 Arrange a wide circle of tomato rounds on a serving platter and set aside.

3 Make the dressing by mixing all the ingredients together in a bowl and set aside.

4 Add some water to the bowl with the salted radish and use your fingers to squeeze the radish in order to help rinse out the salt. Lift out the radish in scoops, squeeze it as dry as possible and then place in the dressing bowl.

5 When all the radish is transferred, mix well and arrange on the platter in the centre of the tomato circle, garnish with chilli and coriander leaves to serve.

roasted eggplant salad
ensaladang talong

Similar to the North African *meschouia*, variants of this are to be found throughout Southeast Asia. This was especially good, though my judgement may have been influenced by my surroundings – the palm-fringed beach, the sun-dappled water...

mixed seasonal salad
2 large purple aubergines
2 garlic cloves, finely chopped
1 medium onion, finely chopped
1 large tomato, finely diced
1 small green sweet pepper, deseeded and finely diced
2 tablespoons white vinegar
1 tablespoon olive oil
1 teaspoon sweet soy sauce
1 teaspoon honey
½ teaspoon grated ginger
ground black pepper
1 teaspoon dry-fried sesame seeds (see page 23)

1 Preheat a hot grill. Arrange the salad leaves on a serving platter and set aside.

2 Grill the aubergines until their skin blacken. When cool enough to handle, peel away the skin, then place the flesh in a bowl and mash it with a fork. Add all the other ingredients and mix well.

3 Turn the contents of the bowl out on to the platter at the centre of the salad leaves and serve.

aubergine, bitter melon and chilli in a vinegar and palm sugar dressing
atsarang talong at ampalaya

1 small bitter melon
5 round green aubergines (see page 19), quartered
mixed seasonal salad

for the marinade
5 tablespoons white vinegar
1 tablespoon palm sugar
1 large red chilli, thinly sliced
6 small garlic cloves, halved lengthwise
4 small shallots, roughly chopped
1 level tablespoon ginger that has been cut into fine matchsticks

1 First make the marinade: in a large bowl, mix the vinegar and palm sugar and stir until the sugar dissolves. Stir in all the other marinade ingredients and mix well.

2 Halve the bitter melon lengthwise, scoop out the seeds, then cut it across into crescents about 5mm (¼in) thick. Add these to the marinade together with the aubergines. Leave to marinate for 1 hour, stirring occasionally.

3 At the end of this time, arrange the salad leaves in a bowl, pour over the contents of the bowl, mix well and serve.

fresh tuna pickled in lime juice with ginger, chilli, onion and sweet pepper

kinilaw na tambakol

At the Amanpulo resort (see page 131) this was made with yellow fin tuna and calamansi juice (see opposite), but I've simplified it here.

mixed seasonal salad
175g (6 oz) fresh tuna, cut into 2.5cm (1in) cubes

for the dressing
3 tablespoons lime juice
1 tablespoon sugar
2 garlic cloves, finely chopped
2 small red chillies, finely chopped
1 level teaspoon grated ginger
1 level teaspoon finely grated lime peel
salt and pepper

1 Arrange the mixed seasonal salad on a serving platter and set aside.

2 Make the dressing by mixing all the ingredients together in a bowl with salt and pepper to taste.

3 Add the cubed tuna to the bowl of dressing, turn the contents well and pour them on to the salad.

Vintas, traditional painted boats, fishing for seashells at Zamboanga

pomelo salad ensaladang suha

The calamansi is a mandarin/kumquat hybrid resembling a lime in appearance and flavour, although it is exceptionally sour. I have put a lot of ordinary lime juice into this recipe to try to achieve the same effect. You may find your pomelo is rather sweet and, if so, you should add even more lime juice to compensate.

1 pomelo, peeled, broken into segments and the pips removed
1 large red chilli, sliced lengthwise into thin matchsticks
1 carrot, sliced into thin matchsticks
2 spring onions, thinly sliced
1 tablespoon lime juice
2 teaspoons sugar
salt and pepper

1 Mix all the ingredients together in a bowl, turn out on to a platter and serve.

corn, sweet pepper and crab meat salad ensaladang mais at siling makupa na may alimasag

This dish was served with pieces of pork crackling, which can easily be bought, ready-cooked, in packets.

60g (2oz) cooked crab meat
1 small onion, finely chopped
2 large garlic cloves, finely chopped
100g (4oz) cooked sweetcorn kernels
2 small sweet peppers (1 green and 1 red), deseeded and finely diced
2 spring onions, thinly sliced

2 tablespoons coconut cream
1 level teaspoon grated ginger
1 level tablespoon finely chopped coriander
2 small red chillies, finely chopped
salt and pepper

1 In a bowl, mix the crab meat with onion and garlic. Set aside.

2 In another bowl, mix all the remaining ingredients with salt and pepper to taste. Turn out on to a serving platter, arrange the crab at the centre and serve.

tomato salad with fresh coriander leaves and cottage cheese wansoy kamatisa at kesong puti

3 large tomatoes, thinly sliced
150g (5oz) cottage cheese
1 heaped tablespoon finely chopped fresh coriander leaves

for the dressing
2 tablespoons olive oil
1 teaspoon honey
2 tablespoons lemon juice
½ teaspoon salt
¼ teaspoon ground black pepper

1 Arrange the tomatoes on a serving platter and spoon over the cottage cheese. Sprinkle with chopped coriander leaves and set aside.

2 Make the dressing by mixing together all the ingredients well. Pour the dressing over the salad and serve.

watercress salad with salty egg
pako at itlon na maalat

The original for this dish is a speciality of the Bistro Remedios, by most accounts the best Filipino restaurant in Manila. There it is made with what the owners call 'fern', a plant seemingly unique to the islands. I've worked out my own version using watercress. The salty eggs are really easy to make, but you have to start three weeks ahead of making this dish and you'll need a large preserving jar with a rubber seal. You only need two salty eggs for this dish, but it seemed wasteful not to make more at the same time. The rest can be boiled or fried and served with a curry or another salad.

150g (5oz) watercress
2 large tomatoes, thinly sliced
4 small shallots, thinly sliced

for the salty eggs
8 ducks' eggs
300g (10 oz) salt

for the dressing
2 tablespoons white vinegar
2 tablespoons fish sauce
2 teaspoons sugar
2 small red chillies, finely chopped

1 At least 3 weeks ahead, prepare the salty eggs: place the eggs in a large preserving jar, taking care not to crack the shells. Heat 700ml (1¼ pint) water in a pan with the salt until it dissolves. Allow to cool, then pour over the eggs and seal the jar. Leave for 3 weeks.

2 Hard-boil 2 salty eggs. When cool, shell and dice into small cubes. Next arrange the watercress, tomatoes, salty eggs and shallots on a serving platter.

3 Make the dressing by mixing all the ingredients together in a bowl, stirring until the sugar dissolves. Pour over the salad, mix well and serve.

jack fruit salad
ensaladang langka

The delicious jack fruit is now fairly easy to find in the West, though it seems to be little used other than by those originally from the countries from which it is imported. This is mainly because most are so big that an individual – even a couple – would have difficulty consuming a whole one themselves. It is also quite tricky to peel, stone and break up into its rich golden segments. Some Asian stores do sell packets of prepared jack fruit segments, but if you can't find them then settle for canned. You'll have to wash away as much of the syrup as you can, but the rather chewy fruit holds up well to the canning process. This salad goes well with some firm salad leaves, say Cos lettuce.

150g (5oz) jack fruit segments, torn lengthwise into thin shreds
2 small sweet peppers (1 red and 1 green), deseeded and finely diced
1 small onion, finely chopped

for the dressing
2 tablespoons vegetable oil
1 teaspoon mild mustard (Dijon or similar)
1 teaspoon honey
salt and pepper

1 In a bowl, mix all the salad ingredients and set aside.

2 Prepare the dressing: place all the dressing ingredients in a small bowl with salt and pepper to taste and whisk together until well mixed.

3 Pour the dressing over the salad and mix well.

salad of water spinach stems spiced with chillies in coconut cream

gising gising

150g (5oz) water spinach (morning glory, see page 22)

2 tablespoons cooking oil

2 garlic cloves, finely chopped

85g (3oz) minced pork

85g (3oz) chopped prawn

2 tablespoons fish sauce

2 teaspoons sugar

4 tablespoons coconut cream

2 small red or green chillies, finely chopped

1 Bring a pan of water to the boil. Discard any leaves from the water spinach and cut the stems into 1cm (½in) rounds. Briefly blanch these stems in the boiling water and drain well. Arrange on a platter and set aside

2 Heat the oil in a frying pan or wok and fry the garlic until golden brown. Add the pork, stir well and simmer until cooked through, about 2 – 3 minutes. Then add the chopped prawn and mix well. Add all the remaining ingredients and stir well.

3 Pour over the water spinach stems and serve.

Spit-roasting pigs, Manila

crisp cubes of green mango served with spicy shrimp paste
ensalada paborito

Everyone has to go to one of the Kamayan restaurants at some point – they're part of the folklore of Philippine dining. I chose the branch on Manila's Padre Faura Street. Their name means 'bare hands' and there are rows of water jars to wash at before eating traditional-style. This is something of a test, as you are virtually obliged to eat the traditional spit-roasted pig, which is nothing if not greasy. To counterbalance the fat I would suggest this salad – or, better still, just have the salad...

1 green (raw) mango, peeled and cut into 1cm (½in) cubes
1 onion, cut into 1cm (½in) cubes
1 large tomato, cut into 1cm (½in) cubes

for the dressing
1 teaspoon shrimp paste
2 garlic cloves, finely chopped
1 tablespoon fish sauce
1 tablespoon lemon juice
2 teaspoons sugar
¼ teaspoon chilli powder
1 level tablespoon ground dried shrimp

1 In a bowl, mix all the salad ingredients and set aside.

2 Prepare the dressing: preheat a hot grill. Wrap the shrimp paste in foil and grill the foil parcel for 1 minute on each side. Mix the grilled shrimp paste together with all the remaining dressing ingredients in another bowl, stirring well.

3 Pour the dressing over the salad, mix well and serve.

sweet potato and chicken salad
camote manok ensalada

A Filipina friend tells me that this dish is one of the most 'Spanish' survivors in the local culinary repertoire. It certainly doesn't require any Eastern flavourings and could be made anywhere on the Mediterranean.

150g (5oz) sweet potato
85g (3oz) carrots
1 onion, roughly diced
2 cooked skinless chicken breast fillets, finely shredded (see page 23)
6 Cos lettuce leaves, roughly shredded

for the dressing
3 tablespoons lemon juice
½ teaspoon ground black pepper
salt

1 Bring a pan of water to the boil. Peel the sweet potato and carrots and then cut them into 1cm (½in) cubes. Boil the carrot cubes for 5 minutes and the sweet potato for 5 to 7 minutes, until just tender but still firm. Drain well and put in a bowl. Add the onion and the shredded chicken, mix well and set aside.

2 Arrange the lettuce leaves on a serving platter and set aside.

3 Make the dressing by mixing the ingredients together well in a small bowl with salt to taste.

4 Pour the dressing into the bowl with the chicken mixture and stir well. Turn out on to the lettuce leaves and serve.

mixed cooked vegetable salad
halo luto gulay ensalada

3 carrots, cut into thin matchsticks
100g (4oz) French beans, halved
100g (4oz) cauliflower, broken into florets
100g (4oz) bamboo shoots
100g (4oz) okra, cut at an angle into 2.5cm (1in) lengths
60g (2oz) beansprouts
1 teaspoon salt
2 tablespoons dry-fried sesame seeds
2 tablespoons crisp-fried shallots (see page 23)
2 tablespoons groundnut oil

1 Bring a pan of water to the boil and briefly blanch each vegetable in turn, ensuring they remain firm: the carrots for the longest (about 5 minutes); the beansprouts the briefest (about 30 seconds). Drain each well and place in a serving bowl.

2 When all the vegetables are in the bowl, add all the remaining ingredients, stir well and serve.

Following pages: Fish farm, Songkhla, southern Thailand

index